M000036502

Laura

Happy 2002

We love Ya

Dad and Mom

Bible Promises
to Treasure
for Women

Inspiring

words

for every

occasion

BROADMAN
&HOLMAN
PUBLISHERS

Nashville, Tennessee

Bible Promises
to Treasure
for Women

Bible Promises to Treasure for Women
©1998 Broadman & Holman Publishers,
Nashville, Tennessee
All rights reserved
Printed in Belgium

ISBN 0-8054-9329-8

Dewey Decimal Classification: 248.8
Subject Heading: CHRISTIAN WOMEN

******

A note on the sources of quotations. When possible I have supplied at least the book name from which contemporary quotes have come. Yet even this is often impossible, since many came from my "journal of jottings" over many years. Also, if a quote is from a person who lived longer than fifty or so years ago, I've made no attempt to cite the source. Such quotations are usually available in any standard book of quotes.

******

Library of Congress Cataloging-in-Publication Data
Bible promises to treasure for women : inspiring words for every occasion / compiled by Gary Wilde.
    p. cm.
  Includes bibliographical references.
  ISBN 0-8054-9329-8
  1. Christian women—Religious life. 2. Christian life—Quotations maxims, etc.   I. Wilde, Gary
BV4527.B55 1999
248.8'43—dc21   98-36027
                                                                    CIP

2 3 4 5 6 02 01 00 99

Contents

—Four—

Facing Daily Stress? 59

—Five—

Seeking Peace Inside? 76

Introduction

I remember as a child singing often at church: "Standing on the Promises of God." Or maybe it was mostly the adults who were singing; but I was standing next to them—my parents and all the others. I recall those faithful people joyfully reciting words they must surely have known by heart . . .

When the howling storms
of doubt and fear assail,
By the living Word of God I shall prevail,
Standing on the promises of God.

For years Downey Church, in sunny central Florida, had preached and taught the promises of God and believed in His goodness. From the beginning—when the church building was a

1

small tin-roofed, A-frame at the east end of a dirt road on the outskirts of Orlando—people would gather to stand on the immutable promises. Under the shiny tin roof, standing on the sandy-wooden floorboards, they melded their voices to the tunes of the upright piano and recalled God's goodness. Today, as the church there grows and thrives—now there is also a school and gymnasium—I can only attribute its vibrant life to a love of God's promises and the recognition that without the pledges that flow from the mouth of God, there is no church, no music, and no reason for either.

The promises of God have always been the bedrock of Christian faith; for without God's sacred covenants with us, we cannot survive. In times of joy or heartache, in all our ups and downs, we keep coming back to that source of our life: the motivation for all our doing and the reason for our existence. It is the message of

God's mighty assurances: this life is not all there is, He will always be with us while we are here, and He will take us to be with Him someday. Yes, we do have priceless promises to keep close to our hearts!

My hope for you as you delve into this scriptural treasure chest is that you will grow deeper in love with the One who has spoken as no other ever could. With so many influences bombarding our minds each moment of the day, what could be better than to set aside a few moments of quiet to hear the still, small voice that constantly invites us into warm fellowship? We'll be richly rewarded if we truly listen to what that voice is saying. His words convey blessing and guidance, wisdom and warning, life for now and life everlasting. What incomparable grace!

Gary Wilde
Oviedo, Florida, 1998

Yes, you know your name, and you know where you're from. But do you know who you are in the universe? You are a creature of the Almighty Creator. You are a child of the King! Are you living like it?

First and Foremost: You Are Blessed!

Once you understand that God is the center of the universe, it's all very simple. Not a day goes by that I don't say, "Thank you. I'm truly blessed."

—*Oprah Winfrey*[1]

He that toucheth you toucheth the apple of his eye.

—*Zechariah 2:8*

And [Jesus] lifted up his hands, and blessed them.

—*Luke 24:50*

And God blessed them, and God said unto them, Be fruitful, and multiply, and replenish the earth, and subdue it: and have dominion over the fish of the sea, and over the fowl of the air, and over every living thing that moveth upon the earth.

And God saw every thing that he had made, and, behold, it was very good. And the evening and the morning were the sixth day.

—*Genesis 1:28, 31*

The grace of our Lord Jesus Christ be with your spirit. Amen.

—*Galatians 6:18*

Remember Who You Are in Christ . . .

My song shall be of Jesus.
When sitting at his feet,
I call to mind his goodness
And know my joy's complete.
My song shall be of Jesus.
Whatever ills befall,
I'll sing the grace that saves me,
And triumphs over all.

—*Fanny J. Crosby*

For mine eyes have seen thy salvation,
Which thou hast prepared before the face
of all people.

—*Luke 2:30–31*

🐂 *You've Been Redeemed from Sin*

He sent redemption unto his people: he
hath commanded his covenant for ever:
holy and reverend is his name.

—*Psalm 111:9*

Let Israel hope in the LORD: for with the
LORD there is mercy, and with him is
plenteous redemption.

—*Psalm 130:7*

Even as the Son of man came not to be
ministered unto, but to minister, and to give
his life a ransom for many.

—*Matthew 20:28*

Being justified freely by his grace through
the redemption that is in Christ Jesus.

—*Romans 3:24*

But of him are ye in Christ Jesus, who of God is made unto us wisdom, and righteousness, and sanctification, and redemption.

—1 Corinthians 1:30

For ye are bought with a price: therefore glorify God in your body, and in your spirit, which are God's.

—1 Corinthians 6:20

I am crucified with Christ: nevertheless I live; yet not I, but Christ liveth in me: and the life which I now live in the flesh I live by the faith of the Son of God, who loved me, and gave himself for me.

—Galatians 2:20

✿ *You Are Forgiven*

For this is my blood of the new testament, which is shed for many for the remission of sins.

—Matthew 26:28

And you, being dead in your sins and the uncircumcision of your flesh, hath he quickened together with him, having forgiven you all trespasses.

—*Colossians 2:13*

For I will be merciful to their unrighteousness, and their sins and their iniquities will I remember no more.

—*Hebrews 8:12*

But if we walk in the light, as he is in the light, we have fellowship one with another, and the blood of Jesus Christ his Son cleanseth us from all sin.

If we say that we have no sin, we deceive ourselves, and the truth is not in us.

If we confess our sins, he is faithful and just to forgive us our sins, and to cleanse us from all unrighteousness.

—*1 John 1:7–9*

My little children, these things write I unto you, that ye sin not. And if any man sin, we have an advocate with the Father, Jesus Christ the righteous:

And he is the propitiation for our sins: and not for ours only, but also for the sins of the whole world. . . .

I write unto you, little children, because your sins are forgiven you for his name's sake.

—*1 John 2:1–2, 12*

If they shall confess their iniquity, and the iniquity of their fathers, with their trespass which they trespassed against me, and that also they have walked contrary unto me;

And that I also have walked contrary unto them, and have brought them into the land of their enemies; if then their uncircumcised hearts be humbled, and they then accept of the punishment of their iniquity:

Then will I remember my covenant with Jacob, and also my covenant with Isaac, and also my covenant with Abraham will I remember; and I will remember the land.

—*Leviticus 26:40–42*

If my people, which are called by my name, shall humble themselves, and pray, and seek my face, and turn from their wicked ways; then will I hear from heaven, and will forgive their sin, and will heal their land.

—*2 Chronicles 7:14*

ও You've Been Born Anew

Jesus answered and said unto him, Verily, verily, I say unto thee, Except a man be born again, he cannot see the kingdom of God.

Nicodemus saith unto him, How can a man be born when he is old? can he enter the second time into his mother's womb, and be born?

Jesus answered, Verily, verily, I say unto thee, Except a man be born of water and of the Spirit, he cannot enter into the kingdom of God.

That which is born of the flesh is flesh; and that which is born of the Spirit is spirit.

Marvel not that I said unto thee, Ye must be born again.

The wind bloweth where it listeth, and thou hearest the sound thereof, but canst not tell whence it cometh, and whither it goeth: so is every one that is born of the Spirit.

—*John 3:3–8*

Seeing ye have purified your souls in obeying the truth through the Spirit unto unfeigned love of the brethren, see that ye love one another with a pure heart fervently:

Being born again, not of corruptible seed, but of incorruptible, by the word of God, which liveth and abideth for ever.

—*1 Peter 1:22–23*

✂ You're Adopted as God's Child

And Jesus called a little child unto him.

—*Matthew 18:2*

For as many as are led by the Spirit of God, they are the sons of God.

For ye have not received the spirit of bondage again to fear; but ye have received the Spirit of adoption, whereby we cry, Abba, Father.

The Spirit itself beareth witness with our spirit, that we are the children of God:

And if children, then heirs; heirs of God, and joint-heirs with Christ; if so be that we suffer with him, that we may be also glorified together.

For I reckon that the sufferings of this present time are not worthy to be compared with the glory which shall be revealed in us.

For the earnest expectation of the creature waiteth for the manifestation of the sons of God.

For the creature was made subject to vanity, not willingly, but by reason of him who hath subjected the same in hope,

Because the creature itself also shall be delivered from the bondage of corruption into the glorious liberty of the children of God. . . . .

For whom he did foreknow, he also did predestinate to be conformed to the image of his Son, that he might be the firstborn among many brethren.

—*Romans 8:14–21, 29*

❧ You Are Perfectly Sanctified

Sanctify them through thy truth: thy word is truth.

As thou hast sent me into the world, even so have I also sent them into the world.

And for their sakes I sanctify myself, that they also might be sanctified through the truth.

—John 17:17–19

Now he which stablisheth us with you in Christ, and hath anointed us, is God;

Who hath also sealed us, and given the earnest of the Spirit in our hearts.

—2 Corinthians 1:21–22

Blessed be the God and Father of our Lord Jesus Christ, who hath blessed us with all spiritual blessings in heavenly places in Christ:

According as he hath chosen us in him before the foundation of the world, that we should be holy and without blame before him in love.

—*Ephesians 1:3–4*

For this is the will of God, even your sanctification, that ye should abstain from fornication:

That every one of you should know how to possess his vessel in sanctification and honour.

—*1 Thessalonians 4:3–4*

So . . . Are You Growing in the Faith?

If it can be verified, we don't need faith. . . . Faith is for that which lies on the other side of reason. Faith is what makes life bearable, with all its tragedies and ambiguities and sudden, startling joys.

—*Madeleine L'Engle*[2]

Trust in the LORD with all thine heart; and lean not unto thine own understanding.

In all thy ways acknowledge him, and he shall direct thy paths.

—Proverbs 3:5–6

When thou liest down, thou shalt not be afraid: yea, thou shalt lie down, and thy sleep shall be sweet.

Be not afraid of sudden fear, neither of the desolation of the wicked, when it cometh.

For the LORD shall be thy confidence, and shall keep thy foot from being taken.

—Proverbs 3:24–26

For I know that my redeemer liveth, and that he shall stand at the latter day upon the earth:

And though after my skin worms destroy this body, yet in my flesh shall I see God:

Whom I shall see for myself, and mine eyes shall behold, and not another; though my reins be consumed within me.

—Job 19:25–27

Although the fig tree shall not blossom, neither shall fruit be in the vines; the labour of the olive shall fail, and the fields shall yield no meat; the flock shall be cut off from the fold, and there shall be no herd in the stalls:

Yet I will rejoice in the LORD, I will joy in the God of my salvation.

The LORD God is my strength, and he will make my feet like hinds' feet, and he will make me to walk upon mine high places. To the chief singer on my stringed instruments.

—*Habakkuk 3:17–19*

Then saith he to Thomas, reach hither thy finger, and behold my hands; and reach hither thy hand, and thrust it into my side: and be not faithless, but believing.

And Thomas answered and said unto him, My Lord and my God.

Jesus saith unto him, Thomas, because thou hast seen me, thou hast believed: blessed are they that have not seen, and yet have believed.

And many other signs truly did Jesus in the presence of his disciples, which are not written in this book:

But these are written, that ye might believe that Jesus is the Christ, the Son of God; and that believing ye might have life through his name.

—*John 20:27–31*

For they themselves shew of us what manner of entering in we had unto you, and how ye turned to God from idols to serve the living and true God.

—*1 Thessalonians 1:9*

Two

Wanting More Love in Your Life?

Love is the great treasure of life—having someone to love and having someone to love us back. And though it seems we never have enough of love (because it comes and goes as people around us decide to extend or withhold it), we can focus on the one Source of love that will never dry up: the heart of God.

Are You Single and Lonely?

The whole conviction of my life now rests upon the belief that loneliness, far from being a rare and curious phenomenon, peculiar to myself and to a few other solitary [persons], is the central and inevitable fact of human existence.

—Thomas Wolfe

My God, my God, why hast thou forsaken me? why art thou so far from helping me, and from the words of my roaring?

O my God, I cry in the daytime, but thou hearest not; and in the night season, and am not silent.

But thou art holy, O thou that inhabitest the praises of Israel.

Our fathers trusted in thee: they trusted, and thou didst deliver them.

They cried unto thee, and were delivered: they trusted in thee, and were not confounded.

But I am a worm, and no man; a reproach of men, and despised of the people.

All they that see me laugh me to scorn: they shoot out the lip, they shake the head, saying,

He trusted on the LORD that he would deliver him: let him deliver him, seeing he delighted in him.

—*Psalm 22:1–8*

For a small moment have I forsaken thee; but with great mercies will I gather thee.

—*Isaiah 54:7*

And they continued stedfastly in the apostles' doctrine and fellowship, and in breaking of bread, and in prayers.

And fear came upon every soul: and many wonders and signs were done by the apostles.

And all that believed were together, and had all things common;

And sold their possessions and goods, and parted them to all men, as every man had need.

And they, continuing daily with one accord in the temple, and breaking bread from house to house, did eat their meat with gladness and singleness of heart,

Praising God, and having favour with all the people. And the Lord added to the church daily such as should be saved.

—Acts 2:42–47

For ye are all the children of God by faith in Christ Jesus.

For as many of you as have been baptized into Christ have put on Christ.

There is neither Jew nor Greek, there is neither bond nor free, there is neither male nor female: for ye are all one in Christ Jesus.

—Galatians 3:26–28

Love Is Here for You— Always!

*May the power of your love, O Lord,
fiery and sweet as honey,
wean my heart from all*

that is under heaven,
so that I may die for love of your love,
you who were so good
as to die for love of my love.

—*St. Francis of Assisi*

But God commendeth his love toward us,
in that, while we were yet sinners, Christ
died for us.

—*Romans 5:8*

And we know that all things work
together for good to them that love God, to
them who are the called according to his
purpose.

For whom he did foreknow, he also did
predestinate to be conformed to the image
of his Son, that he might be the firstborn
among many brethren.

Moreover whom he did predestinate,
them he also called: and whom he called,
them he also justified: and whom he
justified, them he also glorified.

What shall we then say to these things? If
God be for us, who can be against us?

He that spared not his own Son, but delivered him up for us all, how shall he not with him also freely give us all things?

Who shall lay any thing to the charge of God's elect? It is God that justifieth.

Who is he that condemneth? It is Christ that died, yea rather, that is risen again, who is even at the right hand of God, who also maketh intercession for us.

—*Romans 8:28–34*

Who shall separate us from the love of Christ? shall tribulation, or distress, or persecution, or famine, or nakedness, or peril, or sword?

As it is written, For thy sake we are killed all the day long; we are accounted as sheep for the slaughter.

Nay, in all these things we are more than conquerors through him that loved us.

For I am persuaded, that neither death, nor life, nor angels, nor principalities, nor powers, nor things present, nor things to come,

Nor height, nor depth, nor any other creature, shall be able to separate us from the love of God, which is in Christ Jesus our Lord.

—*Romans 8:35–39*

Are You Married?

Marriage resembles a pair of shears, so joined that they cannot be separated; often moving in opposite directions, yet always punishing any one who comes between them.

—*Sydney Smith*

So God created man in his own image, in the image of God created he him; male and female created he them.

—*Genesis 1:27*

And the LORD God said, It is not good that the man should be alone; I will make him an help meet for him.

And out of the ground the LORD God formed every beast of the field, and every fowl of the air; and brought them unto

Adam to see what he would call them: and whatsoever Adam called every living creature, that was the name thereof.

And Adam gave names to all cattle, and to the fowl of the air, and to every beast of the field; but for Adam there was not found an help meet for him.

And the LORD God caused a deep sleep to fall upon Adam, and he slept: and he took one of his ribs, and closed up the flesh instead thereof;

And the rib, which the LORD God had taken from man, made he a woman, and brought her unto the man.

And Adam said, This is now bone of my bones, and flesh of my flesh: she shall be called Woman, because she was taken out of Man.

Therefore shall a man leave his father and his mother, and shall cleave unto his wife: and they shall be one flesh.

And they were both naked, the man and his wife, and were not ashamed.

—Genesis 2:18–25

So Boaz took Ruth, and she was his wife: and when he went in unto her, the LORD gave her conception, and she bare a son.

And the women said unto Naomi, Blessed be the LORD, which hath not left thee this day without a kinsman, that his name may be famous in Israel.

And he shall be unto thee a restorer of thy life, and a nourisher of thine old age: for thy daughter in law, which loveth thee, which is better to thee than seven sons, hath born him.

—Ruth 4:13–15

When a man hath taken a new wife, he shall not go out to war, neither shall he be charged with any business: but he shall be free at home one year, and shall cheer up his wife which he hath taken.

—Deuteronomy 24:5

Marriage is honourable in all, and the bed undefiled.

—Hebrews 13:4

Single or Married, Avoid Sexual Sin

The act of marriage is that beautiful and intimate relationship shared uniquely by a husband and wife in the privacy of their love—and it is sacred. In a real sense, God designed them for that relationship.

—Tim and Beverly LaHaye

For this is the will of God, even your sanctification, that ye should abstain from fornication:

That every one of you should know how to possess his vessel in sanctification and honour;

Not in the lust of concupiscence, even as the Gentiles which know not God:

That no man go beyond and defraud his brother in any matter: because that the Lord is the avenger of all such, as we also have forewarned you and testified.

For God hath not called us unto uncleanness, but unto holiness.

He therefore that despiseth, despiseth not man, but God, who hath also given unto us his holy Spirit.

—1 Thessalonians 4:3–8

Flee also youthful lusts: but follow righteousness, faith, charity, peace, with them that call on the Lord out of a pure heart.

—2 Timothy 2:22

Ye have heard that it was said by them of old time, Thou shalt not commit adultery:

But I say unto you, That whosoever looketh on a woman to lust after her hath committed adultery with her already in his heart.

—Matthew 5:27–28

Reckon ye also yourselves to be dead indeed unto sin, but alive unto God through Jesus Christ our Lord.

Let not sin therefore reign in your mortal body, that ye should obey it in the lusts thereof.

Neither yield ye your members as instruments of unrighteousness unto sin: but yield yourselves unto God, as those that are alive from the dead, and your members as instruments of righteousness unto God.

For sin shall not have dominion over you: for ye are not under the law, but under grace.

—*Romans 6:11–14*

Lonely or Not, Keep Reaching Out

People are lonely because they build walls instead of bridges.

—*Joseph F. Newton*

Bear ye one another's burdens, and so fulfil the law of Christ.

For if a man think himself to be something, when he is nothing, he deceiveth himself.

But let every man prove his own work, and then shall he have rejoicing in himself alone, and not in another.

—*Galatians 6:2–4*

With all lowliness and meekness, with longsuffering, forbearing one another in love;
Endeavouring to keep the unity of the Spirit in the bond of peace.

—*Ephesians 4:2–3*

Enjoy Your Relationship with God

Melancholy is the poison of devotion. When one is in tribulation, it is necessary to be more happy and more joyful because one is nearer to God.

—*Clare of Assisi*

My soul shall be satisfied as with marrow and fatness; and my mouth shall praise thee with joyful lips.

—*Psalm 63:5*

Whoso trusteth in the LORD, happy is [s]he.

—*Proverbs 16:20*

I delight to do thy will, O my God: yea, thy law is within my heart.

—*Psalm 40:8*

They shall be abundantly satisfied with the fatness of thy house; and thou shalt make them drink of the river of thy pleasures.

—*Psalm 36:8*

Blessed is every one that feareth the LORD; that walketh in his ways.

For thou shalt eat the labour of thine hands: happy shalt thou be, and it shall be well with thee.

—*Psalm 128:1–2*

Happy is that people, that is in such a case: yea, happy is that people, whose God is the LORD.

—*Psalm 144:15*

Let Worship Fill Your Soul!

So many things will offer themselves to me for "worship" today. But reveal Yourself, God, in all Your creativity, as the only Being worthy of my true adoration.

—*Gary Wilde*[1]

Praise ye the LORD. Praise ye the name of the LORD; praise him, O ye servants of the LORD.

Ye that stand in the house of the LORD, in the courts of the house of our God,

Praise the LORD; for the LORD is good: sing praises unto his name; for it is pleasant.

—*Psalm 135:1–3*

I will praise thee with my whole heart: before the gods will I sing praise unto thee.

—*Psalm 138:1*

I will speak of the glorious honour of thy majesty, and of thy wondrous works.

And men shall speak of the might of thy terrible acts: and I will declare thy greatness.

The LORD is righteous in all his ways, and holy in all his works.

The LORD is nigh unto all them that call upon him, to all that call upon him in truth.

He will fulfil the desire of them that fear him: he also will hear their cry, and will save them.

The LORD preserveth all them that love him: but all the wicked will he destroy.

My mouth shall speak the praise of the LORD: and let all flesh bless his holy name for ever and ever.

—*Psalm 145:5–6,17–21*

Three

Coping with Tough Times?

Janet's best friend smiled and said, "So, what's the next crisis looming on your horizon?"

It caught Janet by surprise, because the two of them had just successfully solved a significant problem that had been upsetting Janet for months. But as her friend wisely pointed out, we can expect the hard times—always. And perhaps we ought to plan ahead for them.

Made any "crisis plans" lately?

When You're Afraid

There is not a guarantee in the world. Oh, your needs are guaranteed; your needs are absolutely guaranteed by the most stringent of warranties, in the plainest, truest words: knock; seek; ask. But you must read the fine print. "Not as the world giveth, give I unto you."

—*Annie Dillard*[1]

Fear came upon me, and trembling, which made all my bones to shake.

—*Job 4:14*

Be strong and of a good courage, fear not, nor be afraid of them: for the LORD thy God, he it is that doth go with thee; he will not fail thee, nor forsake thee.

—*Deuteronomy 31:6*

Have not I commanded thee? Be strong and of a good courage; be not afraid, neither be thou dismayed: for the LORD thy God is with thee whithersoever thou goest.

—*Joshua 1:9*

The LORD is my light and my salvation; whom shall I fear? the LORD is the strength of my life; of whom shall I be afraid?

When the wicked, even mine enemies and my foes, came upon me to eat up my flesh, they stumbled and fell.

Though an host should encamp against me, my heart shall not fear: though war should rise against me, in this will I be confident.

—*Psalm 27:1–3*

For I have heard the slander of many: fear was on every side: while they took counsel together against me, they devised to take away my life.

—*Psalm 31:13*

Therefore will not we fear, though the earth be removed, and though the mountains be carried into the midst of the sea.

—*Psalm 46:2*

There is no fear in love; but perfect love casteth out fear: because fear hath torment. He that feareth is not made perfect in love.

—*1 John 4:18*

For God hath not given us the spirit of fear; but of power, and of love, and of a sound mind.

—*2 Timothy 1:7*

When You're Worn Out and Exhausted

There are two kinds of weakness, that which breaks and that which bends.

—*Unknown*

Have mercy upon me, O LORD; for I am weak: O LORD, heal me; for my bones are vexed.

My soul is also sore vexed: but thou, O LORD, how long?

—*Psalm 6:2–3*

But God hath chosen the foolish things of the world to confound the wise; and God hath chosen the weak things of the world to confound the things which are mighty.

—*1 Corinthians 1:27*

He giveth power to the faint; and to them that have no might he increaseth strength.

Even the youths shall faint and be weary, and the young men shall utterly fall:

But they that wait upon the LORD shall renew their strength; they shall mount up with wings as eagles; they shall run, and not be weary; and they shall walk, and not faint.

—*Isaiah 40:29–31*

Come unto me, all ye that labour and are heavy laden, and I will give you rest.

Take my yoke upon you, and learn of me; for I am meek and lowly in heart: and ye shall find rest unto your souls.

For my yoke is easy, and my burden is light.

—*Matthew 11:28–30*

And he said unto me, My grace is sufficient for thee: for my strength is made perfect in weakness. Most gladly therefore will I rather glory in my infirmities, that the power of Christ may rest upon me.

Therefore I take pleasure in infirmities, in reproaches, in necessities, in persecutions, in distresses for Christ's sake: for when I am weak, then am I strong.

—2 Corinthians 12:9–10

And let us not be weary in well doing: for in due season we shall reap, if we faint not.

—Galatians 6:9

When You're Overwhelmed with Worry

The misfortunes hardest to bear are these which never came.

—James Russell Lowell

Thou wilt keep him in perfect peace, whose mind is stayed on thee: because he trusteth in thee.

—Isaiah 26:3

For he shall be as a tree planted by the waters, and that spreadeth out her roots by the river, and shall not see when heat cometh, but her leaf shall be green; and shall not be careful in the year of drought, neither shall cease from yielding fruit.

—Jeremiah 17:8

Therefore I say unto you, Take no thought for your life, what ye shall eat, or what ye shall drink; nor yet for your body, what ye shall put on. Is not the life more than meat, and the body than raiment?

—Matthew 6:25

Peace I leave with you, my peace I give unto you: not as the world giveth, give I unto you. Let not your heart be troubled, neither let it be afraid.

—John 14:27

Be careful for nothing; but in every thing by prayer and supplication with thanksgiving let your requests be made known unto God.

And the peace of God, which passeth all understanding, shall keep your hearts and minds through Christ Jesus.

—Philippians 4:6–7

Now the Lord of peace himself give you peace always by all means. The Lord be with you all.

—2 Thessalonians 3:16

When You're Feeling like a Failure

The only time you don't fail is the last time you try anything—and it works.

—William Strong

The LORD is nigh unto them that are of a broken heart; and saveth such as be of a contrite spirit.

—*Psalm 34:18*

Commit thy works unto the LORD, and thy thoughts shall be established.

—*Proverbs 16:3*

But none of these things move me, neither count I my life dear unto myself, so that I might finish my course with joy, and the ministry, which I have received of the Lord Jesus, to testify the gospel of the grace of God.

—*Acts 20:24*

But we have this treasure in earthen vessels, that the excellency of the power may be of God, and not of us.

We are troubled on every side, yet not distressed; we are perplexed, but not in despair;

Persecuted, but not forsaken; cast down, but not destroyed;

Always bearing about in the body the dying of the Lord Jesus, that the life also of Jesus might be made manifest in our body.

For we which live are alway delivered unto death for Jesus' sake, that the life also of Jesus might be made manifest in our mortal flesh.

—2 Corinthians 4:7–11

When You're Frazzled and Stressed-Out

Do not anticipate trouble,
or worry about what may never happen.
Keep in the sunlight.

—Benjamin Franklin

In the day of my trouble I sought the Lord: my sore ran in the night, and ceased not: my soul refused to be comforted.

I remembered God, and was troubled: I complained, and my spirit was overwhelmed.

Thou holdest mine eyes waking: I am so troubled that I cannot speak.

I have considered the days of old, the years of ancient times.

I call to remembrance my song in the night: I commune with mine own heart: and my spirit made diligent search.

—Psalm 77:2–6

I waited patiently for the LORD; and he inclined unto me, and heard my cry.

He brought me up also out of an horrible pit, out of the miry clay, and set my feet upon a rock, and established my goings.

And he hath put a new song in my mouth, even praise unto our God: many shall see it, and fear, and shall trust in the LORD.

—Psalm 40:1–3

Truly my soul waiteth upon God: from him cometh my salvation.

He only is my rock and my salvation; he is my defence; I shall not be greatly moved.

—Psalm 62:1–2

O LORD, thou knowest: remember me, and visit me, and revenge me of my persecutors; take me not away in thy longsuffering: know that for thy sake I have suffered rebuke.

Thy words were found, and I did eat them; and thy word was unto me the joy and rejoicing of mine heart: for I am called by thy name, O LORD God of hosts.

—*Jeremiah 15:15–16*

Who shall also confirm you unto the end, that ye may be blameless in the day of our Lord Jesus Christ.

God is faithful, by whom ye were called unto the fellowship of his Son Jesus Christ our Lord.

—*1 Corinthians 1:8–9*

Rejoice evermore.

Pray without ceasing.

In every thing give thanks: for this is the will of God in Christ Jesus concerning you.

—*1 Thessalonians 5:16–18*

When You're Frustrated

Don't evaluate your life in terms of achievements, trivial or monumental, along the way. If you do, you will be destined to the frustration of always seeking out other destinations, and never allowing yourself actually to be fulfilled. . . . Instead, wake up and appreciate everything you encounter along your path. Enjoy the flowers that are there for your pleasure. Tune in to the sunrise, the little children, the laughter, the rain and the birds. Drink it all in . . . there is no way to happiness; happiness IS the way.

—Dr. Wayne W. Dyer[2]

I will lift up mine eyes unto the hills, from whence cometh my help.

My help cometh from the LORD, which made heaven and earth.

He will not suffer thy foot to be moved: he that keepeth thee will not slumber.

Behold, he that keepeth Israel shall neither slumber nor sleep.

The LORD is thy keeper: the LORD is thy shade upon thy right hand.

The sun shall not smite thee by day, nor the moon by night.

The LORD shall preserve thee from all evil: he shall preserve thy soul.

The LORD shall preserve thy going out and thy coming in from this time forth, and even for evermore.

—*Psalm 121:1–8*

When You Feel Ashamed

It is not the traumas we suffer in childhood which make us emotionally ill, but the inability to express the trauma.

—*John Bradshaw[3]*

Thou hast known my reproach, and my shame, and my dishonour: mine adversaries are all before thee.

—*Psalm 69:19*

My confusion is continually before me,
and the shame of my face hath covered me.

—*Psalm 44:15*

Fear not; for thou shalt not be ashamed:
neither be thou confounded; for thou shalt
not be put to shame: for thou shalt forget
the shame of thy youth, and shalt not
remember the reproach of thy widowhood
any more.

—*Isaiah 54:4*

For your shame ye shall have double; and
for confusion they shall rejoice in their
portion: therefore in their land they shall
possess the double: everlasting joy shall be
unto them.

—*Isaiah 61:7*

And ye shall eat in plenty, and be
satisfied, and praise the name of the LORD
your God, that hath dealt wondrously with
you: and my people shall never be ashamed.
And ye shall know that I am in the midst
of Israel, and that I am the LORD your God,

and none else: and my people shall never be ashamed.

—Joel 2:26–27

As it is written, Behold, I lay in Sion a stumblingstone and rock of offence: and whosoever believeth on him shall not be ashamed.

—Romans 9:33

When You Feel Tempted

It is easier to stay out than get out.

—Mark Twain

But put ye on the Lord Jesus Christ, and make not provision for the flesh, to fulfil the lusts thereof.

—Romans 13:14

The Lord knoweth how to deliver the godly out of temptations.

—2 Peter 2:9

The LORD shall preserve thee from all evil: he shall preserve thy soul.

The LORD shall preserve thy going out and thy coming in from this time forth, and even for evermore.

—Psalm 121:7–8

Put on the whole armour of God, that ye may be able to stand against the wiles of the devil.

For we wrestle not against flesh and blood, but against principalities, against powers, against the rulers of the darkness of this world, against spiritual wickedness in high places.

Wherefore take unto you the whole armour of God, that ye may be able to withstand in the evil day, and having done all, to stand.

Stand therefore, having your loins girt about with truth, and having on the breastplate of righteousness.

—Ephesians 6:11–14

But the Lord is faithful, who shall stablish you, and keep you from evil.

—2 Thessalonians 3:3

For the weapons of our warfare are not carnal, but mighty through God to the pulling down of strong holds.

—2 Corinthians 10:4

And the Lord shall deliver me from every evil work, and will preserve me unto his heavenly kingdom: to whom be glory for ever and ever. Amen.

—2 Timothy 4:18

For in that he himself hath suffered being tempted, he is able to succour them that are tempted.

Wherefore, holy brethren, partakers of the heavenly calling, consider the Apostle and High Priest of our profession, Christ Jesus.

—Hebrews 2:18–3:1

When You're Grieving

Parting after parting
All one's life long;

> *It's a better pang, parting*
> *While love and life are strong.*
> *Parting after parting*
> *Sore fear and sore sore pain*
> *Till one dreads the pang of meeting*
> *More than of parting again.*
>
> —*Christina G. Rossetti*

When I would comfort myself against sorrow, my heart is faint in me.

—*Jeremiah 8:18*

Jesus wept.

—*John 11:35*

Mine eyes do fail with tears, my bowels are troubled, my liver is poured upon the earth, for the destruction of the daughter of my people; because the children and the sucklings swoon in the streets of the city.

They say to their mothers, Where is corn and wine? when they swooned as the wounded in the streets of the city, when their soul was poured out into their mothers' bosom. . . .

Arise, cry out in the night: in the beginning of the watches pour out thine heart like water before the face of the Lord: lift up thy hands toward him for the life of thy young children, that faint for hunger in the top of every street.

—*Lamentations 2:11–12, 19*

When my soul fainted within me I remembered the LORD: and my prayer came in unto thee, into thine holy temple.

—*Jonah 2:7*

Finally, my brethren, be strong in the Lord, and in the power of his might.

—*Ephesians 6:10*

When You're Suffering

We are healed of a suffering only by experiencing it in full.

—*Marcel Proust*

Thou therefore endure hardness, as a good soldier of Jesus Christ. . . .

It is a faithful saying: For if we be dead with him, we shall also live with him:

If we suffer, we shall also reign with him: if we deny him, he also will deny us.

—*2 Timothy 2:3, 11–12*

We are troubled on every side, yet not distressed; we are perplexed, but not in despair;

Persecuted, but not forsaken; cast down, but not destroyed;

Always bearing about in the body the dying of the Lord Jesus, that the life also of Jesus might be made manifest in our body. . . .

For our light affliction, which is but for a moment, worketh for us a far more exceeding and eternal weight of glory;

While we look not at the things which are seen, but at the things which are not seen: for the things which are seen are temporal; but the things which are not seen are eternal.

—*2 Corinthians 4:8–10, 17–18*

But we see Jesus, who was made a little lower than the angels for the suffering of death, crowned with glory and honour; that he by the grace of God should taste death for every man.

For it became him, for whom are all things, and by whom are all things, in bringing many sons unto glory, to make the captain of their salvation perfect through sufferings.

—*Hebrews 2:9–10*

Now no chastening for the present seemeth to be joyous, but grievous: nevertheless afterward it yieldeth the peaceable fruit of righteousness unto them which are exercised thereby.

Wherefore lift up the hands which hang down, and the feeble knees;

And make straight paths for your feet, lest that which is lame be turned out of the way; but let it rather be healed.

—*Hebrews 12:11–13*

But the God of all grace, who hath called us unto his eternal glory by Christ Jesus, after that ye have suffered a while, make you perfect, stablish, strengthen, settle you.

To him be glory and dominion for ever and ever. Amen.

—1 Peter 5:10–11

When You're Angry

Anybody can become angry—that is easy; but to be angry with the right person, and to the right degree, and at the right time, and for the right purpose, and in the right way— that is not within everybody's power and is not easy.

—Aristotle

Be ye angry, and sin not: let not the sun go down upon your wrath.

—Ephesians 4:26

Stand in awe, and sin not: commune with your own heart upon your bed, and be still. Selah.

—Psalm 4:4

Let all bitterness, and wrath, and anger, and clamour, and evil speaking, be put away from you, with all malice.

—*Ephesians 4:31*

Looking diligently lest any man fail of the grace of God; lest any root of bitterness springing up trouble you, and thereby many be defiled.

—*Hebrews 12:15*

But I say unto you, That whosoever is angry with his brother without a cause shall be in danger of the judgment: and whosoever shall say to his brother, Raca, shall be in danger of the council: but whosoever shall say, Thou fool, shall be in danger of hell fire.

—*Matthew 5:22*

—Four—

$\mathcal{F}$acing $\mathcal{D}$aily $\mathcal{S}$tress?

"I know I don't handle stress very well," Carey admitted. *"But I mainly have my parents' example to show me how to react to pressure. And they didn't do very well, either."*

Her friend pointed out that Carey could turn to the wisdom of the Bible for help. After all, the folks we read about there were real people, just like us.

Facing Stressful Times?

*God never built a Christian strong enough
to carry today's duties and tomorrow's
anxieties piled on the top of them.*

—*Theodore Ledyard Cuyler*

Sufficient unto the day is the evil thereof.

—*Matthew 6:34*

Come unto me, all ye that labour and are
heavy laden, and I will give you rest.

Take my yoke upon you, and learn of me;
for I am meek and lowly in heart: and ye
shall find rest unto your souls.

For my yoke is easy, and my burden is
light.

—*Matthew 11:28–30*

Fear thou not; for I am with thee: be not
dismayed; for I am thy God: I will
strengthen thee; yea, I will help thee; yea, I
will uphold thee with the right hand of my
righteousness.

—*Isaiah 41:10*

God is our refuge and strength, a very present help in trouble.

Therefore will not we fear, though the earth be removed, and though the mountains be carried into the midst of the sea;

Though the waters thereof roar and be troubled, though the mountains shake with the swelling thereof.

—*Psalm 46:1–3*

And he was in the hinder part of the ship, asleep on a pillow: and they awake him, and say unto him, Master, carest thou not that we perish?

And he arose, and rebuked the wind, and said unto the sea, Peace, be still. And the wind ceased, and there was a great calm.

And he said unto them, Why are ye so fearful? how is it that ye have no faith?

—*Mark 4:38–40*

Peace I leave with you, my peace I give unto you: not as the world giveth, give I unto you. Let not your heart be troubled, neither let it be afraid.

—*John 14:27*

If the Son therefore shall make you free,
ye shall be free indeed.

—John 8:36

Now it came to pass, as they went, that he
entered into a certain village: and a certain
woman named Martha received him into
her house.

And she had a sister called Mary, which
also sat at Jesus' feet, and heard his word.

But Martha was cumbered about much
serving, and came to him, and said, Lord, dost
thou not care that my sister hath left me to
serve alone? bid her therefore that she help me.

And Jesus answered and said unto her,
Martha, Martha, thou art careful and
troubled about many things:

But one thing is needful: and Mary hath
chosen that good part, which shall not be
taken away from her.

—Luke 10:38–42

For God hath not given us the spirit of
fear; but of power, and of love, and of a
sound mind.

—2 Timothy 1:7

Take Care of Yourself!

You've got to decide on an inner discipline to protect yourself. Step out of the interesting, dynamic rhythm every so often and focus on your internal life. Say, "Stop the world, I want to get off," for a while at least.

—Naomi Rosenblatt

I wish above all things that thou mayest prosper and be in health, even as thy soul prospereth.

—3 John 2

I beseech you therefore, brethren, by the mercies of God, that ye present your bodies a living sacrifice, holy, acceptable unto God, which is your reasonable service.

—Romans 12:1

What? know ye not that your body is the temple of the Holy Ghost which is in you, which ye have of God, and ye are not your own?

For ye are bought with a price: therefore glorify God in your body, and in your spirit, which are God's.

—*1 Corinthians 6:19–20*

He giveth power to the faint; and to them that have no might he increaseth strength.

Even the youths shall faint and be weary, and the young men shall utterly fall:

But they that wait upon the LORD shall renew their strength; they shall mount up with wings as eagles; they shall run, and not be weary; and they shall walk, and not faint.

—*Isaiah 40:29–31*

When thou goest, thy steps shall not be straitened; and when thou runnest, thou shalt not stumble.

—*Proverbs 4:12*

And Remember: The Lord Will Sustain You

Like the fish, swimming in the vast sea and resting in its deeps, and like the bird, boldly mounting high in the sky, so the soul feels its spirit freely moving through the vastness and the depth and the unutterable richnesses of love.

—*Beatrice of Nazareth*

The eternal God is thy refuge, and underneath are the everlasting arms.

—*Deuteronomy 33:27*

For in the time of trouble he shall hide me in his pavilion: in the secret of his tabernacle shall he hide me; he shall set me up upon a rock.

—*Psalm 27:5*

I laid me down and slept; I awaked; for the LORD sustained me.

—*Psalm 3:5*

Seeing he giveth to all life, and breath, and all things;

And hath made of one blood all nations of men for to dwell on all the face of the earth, and hath determined the times before appointed, and the bounds of their habitation;

That they should seek the Lord, if haply they might feel after him, and find him, though he be not far from every one of us:

For in him we live, and move, and have our being . . . For we are also his offspring.

—*Acts 17:25–28*

In the multitude of my thoughts within me thy comforts delight my soul.

—*Psalm 94:19*

For he maketh sore, and bindeth up: he woundeth, and his hands make whole.

—*Job 5:18*

The LORD is my shepherd; I shall not want.

He maketh me to lie down in green pastures: he leadeth me beside the still waters.

He restoreth my soul: he leadeth me in the paths of righteousness for his name's sake.

Yea, though I walk through the valley of the shadow of death, I will fear no evil: for thou art with me; thy rod and thy staff they comfort me.

Thou preparest a table before me in the presence of mine enemies: thou anointest my head with oil; my cup runneth over.

Surely goodness and mercy shall follow me all the days of my life: and I will dwell in the house of the LORD for ever.

—Psalm 23:1–6

Praise ye the LORD: for it is good to sing praises unto our God; for it is pleasant; and praise is comely.

The LORD doth build up Jerusalem: he gathereth together the outcasts of Israel.

He healeth the broken in heart, and bindeth up their wounds.

—Psalm 147:1–3

For I will restore health unto thee, and I will heal thee of thy wounds, saith the LORD; because they called thee an Outcast, saying, This is Zion, whom no man seeketh after.

—*Jeremiah 30:17*

Joyfully Work for Your Creator

I look back on my life like a good day's work.

—*Grandma Moses*

Remember now thy Creator in the days of thy youth, while the evil days come not, nor the years draw nigh, when thou shalt say, I have no pleasure in them;

While the sun, or the light, or the moon, or the stars, be not darkened, nor the clouds return after the rain:

In the day when the keepers of the house shall tremble, and the strong men shall bow themselves, and the grinders cease because they are few, and those that look out of the windows be darkened,

And the doors shall be shut in the streets, when the sound of the grinding is low, and he shall rise up at the voice of the bird, and all the daughters of musick shall be brought low;

Also when they shall be afraid of that which is high, and fears shall be in the way, and the almond tree shall flourish, and the grasshopper shall be a burden, and desire shall fail: because man goeth to his long home, and the mourners go about the streets:

Or ever the silver cord be loosed, or the golden bowl be broken, or the pitcher be broken at the fountain, or the wheel broken at the cistern.

Then shall the dust return to the earth as it was: and the spirit shall return unto God who gave it.

—*Ecclesiastes 12:1–7*

I will praise thee; for I am fearfully and wonderfully made: marvellous are thy works; and that my soul knoweth right well.

My substance was not hid from thee, when I was made in secret, and curiously wrought in the lowest parts of the earth.

Thine eyes did see my substance, yet being unperfect; and in thy book all my members were written, which in continuance were fashioned, when as yet there was none of them.

—*Psalm 139:14–16*

🕊 *Count Your Blessings!*

Behold that which I have seen: it is good and comely for one to eat and to drink, and to enjoy the good of all his labour that he taketh under the sun all the days of his life, which God giveth him: for it is his portion.

Every man also to whom God hath given riches and wealth, and hath given him power to eat thereof, and to take his portion, and to rejoice in his labour; this is the gift of God.

—*Ecclesiastes 5:18–19*

There is nothing better for a man, than that he should eat and drink, and that he should make his soul enjoy good in his labour. This also I saw, that it was from the hand of God.

—*Ecclesiastes 2:24*

And also that every man should eat and drink, and enjoy the good of all his labour, it is the gift of God.

—*Ecclesiastes 3:13*

♔ *Give God the Glory in All Circumstances*

For we are his workmanship, created in Christ Jesus unto good works, which God hath before ordained that we should walk in them.

—*Ephesians 2:10*

That ye might walk worthy of the Lord unto all pleasing, being fruitful in every good work, and increasing in the knowledge of God;

Strengthened with all might, according to his glorious power, unto all patience and longsuffering with joyfulness;

Giving thanks unto the Father, which hath made us meet to be partakers of the inheritance of the saints in light.

—Colossians 1:10–12

ℭ Offer Daily Praise and Thanks

Let the word of Christ dwell in you richly in all wisdom; teaching and admonishing one another in psalms and hymns and spiritual songs, singing with grace in your hearts to the Lord.

—Colossians 3:16

In every thing give thanks: for this is the will of God in Christ Jesus concerning you.

—1 Thessalonians 5:18

O come, let us worship and bow down: let us kneel before the LORD our maker.

—Psalm 95:6

Be careful for nothing; but in every thing by prayer and supplication with thanksgiving let your requests be made known unto God.

—*Philippians 4:6*

The heavens declare the glory of God; and the firmament sheweth his handiwork.

—*Psalm 19:1*

I will sing of the mercies of the LORD for ever: with my mouth will I make known thy faithfulness to all generations.

For I have said, Mercy shall be built up for ever: thy faithfulness shalt thou establish in the very heavens.

I have made a covenant with my chosen, I have sworn unto David my servant,

Thy seed will I establish for ever, and build up thy throne to all generations.

—*Psalm 89:1–4*

The LORD shall increase you more and more, you and your children.

Ye are blessed of the LORD which made heaven and earth.

The heaven, even the heavens, are the
LORD's: but the earth hath he given to the
children of men.

The dead praise not the LORD, neither any
that go down into silence.

But we will bless the LORD from this time
forth and for evermore. Praise the LORD.

—*Psalm 115:14–18*

This is the day which the LORD hath
made; we will rejoice and be glad in it.

—*Psalm 118:24*

I will extol thee, my God, O king; and I
will bless thy name for ever and ever.

Every day will I bless thee; and I will
praise thy name for ever and ever.

Great is the LORD, and greatly to be
praised; and his greatness is unsearchable.

One generation shall praise thy works to
another, and shall declare thy mighty acts.

—*Psalm 145:1–4*

Then saith Jesus unto him, Get thee
hence, Satan: for it is written, Thou shalt

worship the Lord thy God, and him only shalt thou serve.

—Matthew 4:10

Jesus saith unto her, Woman, believe me, the hour cometh, when ye shall neither in this mountain, nor yet at Jerusalem, worship the Father.

Ye worship ye know not what: we know what we worship: for salvation is of the Jews.

But the hour cometh, and now is, when the true worshippers shall worship the Father in spirit and in truth: for the Father seeketh such to worship him.

God is a Spirit: and they that worship him must worship him in spirit and in truth.

—John 4:21–24

Five

Seeking Peace Inside?

Jesus came to give us peace—peace with God and peace within our hearts. But with our hectic schedules and lightning-fast communications, we can live in a state of turmoil, rushing from one activity to the next.

It's time to slow down. And sometimes it's simply a matter of choice: I will be at peace for a few moments. Forgetting what to worry about. Laying aside all the frustrations. Simply basking in God's love and recalling how good are His blessings.

Just Think of the Blessings of This Life!

For all that has been—Thanks!
To all that shall be—Yes!
—*Dag Hammarskjold*

He turneth the wilderness into a standing water, and dry ground into watersprings.

And there he maketh the hungry to dwell, that they may prepare a city for habitation;

And sow the fields, and plant vineyards, which may yield fruits of increase.

He blesseth them also, so that they are multiplied greatly; and suffereth not their cattle to decrease.

—*Psalm 107:35–38*

Except the LORD build the house, they labour in vain that build it: except the LORD keep the city, the watchman waketh but in vain.

It is vain for you to rise up early, to sit up late, to eat the bread of sorrows: for so he giveth his beloved sleep.

Lo, children are an heritage of the LORD: and the fruit of the womb is his reward.

As arrows are in the hand of a mighty man; so are children of the youth.

Happy is the man that hath his quiver full of them: they shall not be ashamed, but they shall speak with the enemies in the gate.

—*Psalm 127:1–5*

Bring ye all the tithes into the storehouse, that there may be meat in mine house, and prove me now herewith, saith the LORD of hosts, if I will not open you the windows of heaven, and pour you out a blessing, that there shall not be room enough to receive it.

And I will rebuke the devourer for your sakes, and he shall not destroy the fruits of your ground; neither shall your vine cast her fruit before the time in the field, saith the LORD of hosts.

And all nations shall call you blessed: for ye shall be a delightsome land, saith the LORD of hosts.

—Malachi 3:10–12

Then There Are the Spiritual Blessings

Now let the soul number its gains and count its treasures. They are so fine that they refine the hands which count them.

—Phillips Brooks

Every good gift and every perfect gift is from above, and cometh down from the Father of lights, with whom is no variableness, neither shadow of turning.

Of his own will begat he us with the word of truth, that we should be a kind of firstfruits of his creatures.

—James 1:17–18

The righteous shall flourish like the palm tree: he shall grow like a cedar in Lebanon.

Those that be planted in the house of the LORD shall flourish in the courts of our God.

They shall still bring forth fruit in old age; they shall be fat and flourishing.

—Psalm 92:12–14

Grace and peace be multiplied unto you through the knowledge of God, and of Jesus our Lord,

According as his divine power hath given unto us all things that pertain unto life and godliness, through the knowledge of him that hath called us to glory and virtue:

Whereby are given unto us exceeding great and precious promises: that by these ye might be partakers of the divine nature, having escaped the corruption that is in the world through lust.

—2 Peter 1:2–4

Blessed be the God and Father of our Lord Jesus Christ, who hath blessed us with all spiritual blessings in heavenly places in Christ.

—Ephesians 1:3

Thy shoes shall be iron and brass; and as thy days, so shall thy strength be.

There is none like unto the God of Jeshurun, who rideth upon the heaven in thy help, and in his excellency on the sky.

The eternal God is thy refuge, and underneath are the everlasting arms.

—*Deuteronomy 33:25–27*

The word that came to Jeremiah from the LORD, saying,

Hear ye the words of this covenant, and speak unto the men of Judah, and to the inhabitants of Jerusalem;

And say thou unto them, Thus saith the LORD God of Israel; Cursed be the man that obeyeth not the words of this covenant,

Which I commanded your fathers in the day that I brought them forth out of the land of Egypt, from the iron furnace, saying, Obey my voice, and do them, according to all which I command you: so shall ye be my people, and I will be your God:

That I may perform the oath which I have sworn unto your fathers, to give them a land flowing with milk and honey, as it is this day. Then answered I, and said, So be it, O LORD.

—Jeremiah 11:1–5

Isn't God Good?

Before me, even as behind,
God is, and all is well.

—John Greenleaf Whittier

The LORD is good, a strong hold in the day of trouble; and he knoweth them that trust in him.

—Nahum 1:7

O LORD our Lord, how excellent is thy name in all the earth! who hast set thy glory above the heavens.

Out of the mouth of babes and sucklings hast thou ordained strength because of thine enemies, that thou mightest still the enemy and the avenger.

When I consider thy heavens, the work of thy fingers, the moon and the stars, which thou hast ordained;

What is man, that thou art mindful of him? and the son of man, that thou visitest him?

For thou hast made him a little lower than the angels, and hast crowned him with glory and honour.

Thou madest him to have dominion over the works of thy hands; thou hast put all things under his feet:

All sheep and oxen, yea, and the beasts of the field;

The fowl of the air, and the fish of the sea, and whatsoever passeth through the paths of the seas.

O LORD our Lord, how excellent is thy name in all the earth!

—Psalm 8:1–9

Good and upright is the LORD: therefore will he teach sinners in the way.

The meek will he guide in judgment: and the meek will he teach his way.

All the paths of the LORD are mercy and truth unto such as keep his covenant and his testimonies.

—*Psalm 25:8–10*

How precious also are thy thoughts unto me, O God! how great is the sum of them!

If I should count them, they are more in number than the sand: when I awake, I am still with thee.

—*Psalm 139:17–18*

Afterward shall the children of Israel return, and seek the LORD their God, and David their king; and shall fear the LORD and his goodness in the latter days.

—*Hosea 3:5*

Or what man is there of you, whom if his son ask bread, will he give him a stone?

Or if he ask a fish, will he give him a serpent?

If ye then, being evil, know how to give good gifts unto your children, how much more shall your Father which is in heaven give good things to them that ask him?

—*Matthew 7:9–11*

Grace be unto you, and peace, from him which is, and which was, and which is to come; and from the seven Spirits which are before his throne;

And from Jesus Christ, who is the faithful witness, and the first begotten of the dead, and the prince of the kings of the earth. Unto him that loved us, and washed us from our sins in his own blood,

And hath made us kings and priests unto God and his Father; to him be glory and dominion for ever and ever. Amen.

—*Revelation 1:4–6*

But Worldly Happiness Will Elude You

Come, O Creator, Spirit blest!
And in our souls take up Thy rest;
Come, with Thy grace and heavenly aid,
To fill the hearts which Thou has made.

—*Mary Artemisia Lathbury*[1]

For I was envious at the foolish, when I saw the prosperity of the wicked. . . .

When I thought to know this, it was too painful for me;

Surely thou didst set them in slippery places: thou castedst them down into destruction.

How are they brought into desolation, as in a moment! they are utterly consumed with terrors.

As a dream when one awaketh; so, O Lord, when thou awakest, thou shalt despise their image.

—*Psalm 73:3, 18–20*

Trust in the LORD, and do good; so shalt thou dwell in the land, and verily thou shalt be fed.

Delight thyself also in the LORD; and he shall give thee the desires of thine heart.

Commit thy way unto the LORD; trust also in him; and he shall bring it to pass.

And he shall bring forth thy righteousness as the light, and thy judgment as the noonday.

Rest in the LORD, and wait patiently for him: fret not thyself because of him who prospereth in his way, because of the man who bringeth wicked devices to pass.

—Psalm 37:3–7

Moreover I will take from them the voice of mirth, and the voice of gladness, the voice of the bridegroom, and the voice of the bride, the sound of the millstones, and the light of the candle.

And this whole land shall be a desolation, and an astonishment; and these nations shall serve the king of Babylon seventy years.

—Jeremiah 25:10–11

And he spake a parable unto them, saying, The ground of a certain rich man brought forth plentifully:

And he thought within himself, saying, What shall I do, because I have no room where to bestow my fruits?

And he said, This will I do: I will pull down my barns, and build greater; and there will I bestow all my fruits and my goods.

And I will say to my soul, Soul, thou hast much goods laid up for many years; take thine ease, eat, drink, and be merry.

But God said unto him, Thou fool, this night thy soul shall be required of thee: then whose shall those things be, which thou hast provided?

—*Luke 12:16–20*

So Seek Spiritual Peace . . .

All the way to heaven is heaven.
—*Catherine of Siena*

Thou shalt make thy prayer unto him, and he shall hear thee, and thou shalt pay thy vows.

Thou shalt also decree a thing, and it shall be established unto thee: and the light shall shine upon thy ways.

When men are cast down, then thou shalt say, There is lifting up; and he shall save the humble person.

He shall deliver the island of the innocent: and it is delivered by the pureness of thine hands.

—*Job 22:27–30*

Dominion and fear are with him, he maketh peace in his high places.

Is there any number of his armies? and upon whom doth not his light arise?

How then can man be justified with God? or how can he be clean that is born of a woman?

Behold even to the moon, and it shineth not; yea, the stars are not pure in his sight.

How much less man, that is a worm? and the son of man, which is a worm?

—*Job 25:2–6*

What man is he that feareth the LORD? him shall he teach in the way that he shall choose.

His soul shall dwell at ease; and his seed shall inherit the earth.

—*Psalm 25:12–13*

The righteous perisheth, and no man layeth it to heart: and merciful men are taken away, none considering that the righteous is taken away from the evil to come.

He shall enter into peace: they shall rest in their beds, each one walking in his uprightness. . . .

I create the fruit of the lips; Peace, peace to him that is far off, and to him that is near, saith the LORD; and I will heal him.

—Isaiah 57:1–2, 19

Now the God of hope fill you with all joy and peace in believing, that ye may abound in hope, through the power of the Holy Ghost. . . .

Now the God of peace be with you all. Amen.

—Romans 15:13, 33

And the peace of God, which passeth all understanding, shall keep your hearts and minds through Christ Jesus.

Finally, brethren, whatsoever things are true, whatsoever things are honest, whatsoever things are just, whatsoever things are pure, whatsoever things are lovely, whatsoever things are of good report; if there be any virtue, and if there be any praise, think on these things.

Those things, which ye have both learned, and received, and heard, and seen in me, do: and the God of peace shall be with you.

—*Philippians 4:7–9*

. . . And Let Contentment Flow In!

All shall be well
and all shall be well
and all manner of thing shall be well.

—*Julian of Norwich*

Godliness with contentment is great gain. For we brought nothing into this world, and it is certain we can carry nothing out.

And having food and raiment let us be therewith content.

—*1 Timothy 6:6–8*

For a day in thy courts is better than a thousand. I had rather be a doorkeeper in the house of my God, than to dwell in the tents of wickedness.

For the LORD God is a sun and shield: the LORD will give grace and glory: no good thing will he withhold from them that walk uprightly.

O LORD of hosts, blessed is the man that trusteth in thee.

—*Psalm 84:10–12*

Two things have I required of thee; deny me them not before I die:

Remove far from me vanity and lies: give me neither poverty nor riches; feed me with food convenient for me:

Lest I be full, and deny thee, and say, Who is the LORD? or lest I be poor, and steal, and take the name of my God in vain.

—*Proverbs 30:7–9*

I know that there is no good in them, but for a man to rejoice, and to do good in his life.

And also that every man should eat and drink, and enjoy the good of all his labour, it is the gift of God.

—*Ecclesiastes 3:12–13*

Behold that which I have seen: it is good and comely for one to eat and to drink, and to enjoy the good of all his labour that he taketh under the sun all the days of his life, which God giveth him: for it is his portion.

Every man also to whom God hath given riches and wealth, and hath given him power to eat thereof, and to take his portion, and to rejoice in his labour; this is the gift of God.

For he shall not much remember the days of his life; because God answereth him in the joy of his heart.

—*Ecclesiastes 5:18–20*

All the labour of man is for his mouth, and yet the appetite is not filled.

For what hath the wise more than the fool? what hath the poor, that knoweth to walk before the living?

Better is the sight of the eyes than the wandering of the desire: this is also vanity and vexation of spirit.

—*Ecclesiastes 6:7–9*

Not that I speak in respect of want: for I have learned, in whatsoever state I am, therewith to be content.

I know both how to be abased, and I know how to abound: every where and in all things I am instructed both to be full and to be hungry, both to abound and to suffer need.

I can do all things through Christ which strengtheneth me.

—*Philippians 4:11–13*

Let your conversation be without covetousness; and be content with such things as ye have: for he hath said, I will never leave thee, nor forsake thee.

—*Hebrews 13:5*

Six

Needing to Make Some Hard Decisions?

Ever been between a rock and a hard place? You know it's no fun! And so many of our decisions seem to put us in the position of having to choose between "the lesser of two evils." Again, not pleasant.

So how do you make decisions like that? Surely knowing the Lord and His Word will help. So consider the passages that follow as you prayerfully face your toughest choices.

From the Start, Give Your Life to the Lord . . .

Take my life and let it be
Consecrated, Lord, to Thee. . . .
Take my hands, and let them move
At the impulse of Thy love.
—*Frances Ridley Havergal*

The sacrifices of God are a broken spirit: a broken and a contrite heart, O God, thou wilt not despise.

—*Psalm 51:17*

And she vowed a vow, and said, O LORD of hosts, if thou wilt indeed look on the affliction of thine handmaid, and remember me, and not forget thine handmaid, but wilt give unto thine handmaid a man child, then I will give him unto the LORD all the days of his life, and there shall no razor come upon his head. . . .

And when she had weaned him, she took him up with her, with three bullocks, and one ephah of flour, and a bottle of wine, and brought him unto the house of the LORD in Shiloh: and the child was young.

And they slew a bullock, and brought the child to Eli.

And she said, Oh my lord, as thy soul liveth, my lord, I am the woman that stood by thee here, praying unto the LORD.

For this child I prayed; and the LORD hath given me my petition which I asked of him:

Therefore also I have lent him to the LORD; as long as he liveth he shall be lent to the LORD. And he worshipped the LORD there.

—*1 Samuel 1:11, 24–28*

Neither yield ye your members as instruments of unrighteousness unto sin: but yield yourselves unto God, as those that are alive from the dead, and your members as instruments of righteousness unto God.

For sin shall not have dominion over you: for ye are not under the law, but under grace.

What then? shall we sin, because we are not under the law, but under grace? God forbid.

Know ye not, that to whom ye yield yourselves servants to obey, his servants ye are to whom ye obey; whether of sin unto death, or of obedience unto righteousness?

But God be thanked, that ye were the servants of sin, but ye have obeyed from the heart that form of doctrine which was delivered you.

Being then made free from sin, ye became the servants of righteousness.

I speak after the manner of men because of the infirmity of your flesh: for as ye have yielded your members servants to uncleanness and to iniquity unto iniquity; even so now yield your members servants to righteousness unto holiness.

—Romans 6:13–19

And this they did, not as we hoped, but first gave their own selves to the Lord, and unto us by the will of God.

—2 Corinthians 8:5

Realize: Life Means Making Choices

When you have to make a choice and don't make it, that in itself is a choice.

—William James

How long halt ye between two opinions? if the LORD be God, follow him: but if Baal, then follow him. And the people answered him not a word.

—1 Kings 18:21

Their heart is divided; now shall they be found faulty: he shall break down their altars, he shall spoil their images.

—Hosea 10:2

No man can serve two masters: for either he will hate the one, and love the other; or else he will hold to the one, and despise the other. Ye cannot serve God and mammon.

—Matthew 6:24

I have set before you life and death, blessing and cursing: therefore choose life, that both thou and thy seed may live.

—Deuteronomy 30:19

Let thine eyes look right on, and let thine eyelids look straight before thee.

Ponder the path of thy feet, and let all thy ways be established.

Turn not to the right hand nor to the left: remove thy foot from evil.

—Proverbs 4:25–27

For the Lord GOD will help me; therefore shall I not be confounded: therefore have I set my face like a flint, and I know that I shall not be ashamed.

—Isaiah 50:7

A double minded man [or woman] is
unstable in all his ways.

—*James 1:8*

Stick with Your Good Decisions

*When possible make the decisions now, even
if action is in the future. A reviewed decision
usually is better than one reached at the last
moment.*

—*William B. Given, Jr.*

That which ye have already hold fast till I
come.

And he that overcometh, and keepeth my
works unto the end, to him will I give
power over the nations.

—*Revelation 2:25–26*

Now we beseech you, brethren, by the
coming of our Lord Jesus Christ, and by our
gathering together unto him,

That ye be not soon shaken in mind, or be troubled, neither by spirit, nor by word, nor by letter as from us, as that the day of Christ is at hand.

Let no man deceive you by any means: for that day shall not come, except there come a falling away first, and that man of sin be revealed, the son of perdition;

Who opposeth and exalteth himself above all that is called God, or that is worshipped; so that he as God sitteth in the temple of God, showing himself that he is God.

Remember ye not, that, when I was yet with you, I told you these things?

And now ye know what withholdeth that he might be revealed in his time.

For the mystery of iniquity doth already work: only he who now letteth will let, until he be taken out of the way.

And then shall that Wicked be revealed, whom the Lord shall consume with the spirit of his mouth, and shall destroy with the brightness of his coming:

Even him, whose coming is after the working of Satan with all power and signs and lying wonders,

And with all deceivableness of unrighteousness in them that perish; because they received not the love of the truth, that they might be saved.

And for this cause God shall send them strong delusion, that they should believe a lie:

That they all might be damned who believed not the truth, but had pleasure in unrighteousness.

But we are bound to give thanks alway to God for you, brethren beloved of the Lord, because God hath from the beginning chosen you to salvation through sanctification of the Spirit and belief of the truth:

Whereunto he called you by our gospel, to the obtaining of the glory of our Lord Jesus Christ.

Therefore, brethren, stand fast, and hold the traditions which ye have been taught, whether by word, or our epistle.

Now our Lord Jesus Christ himself, and God, even our Father, which hath loved us, and hath given us everlasting consolation and good hope through grace,

Comfort your hearts, and stablish you in every good word and work.

—*2 Thessalonians 2:1–17*

Hold fast the form of sound words, which thou hast heard of me, in faith and love which is in Christ Jesus.

That good thing which was committed unto thee keep by the Holy Ghost which dwelleth in us.

—*2 Timothy 1:13–14*

But Christ as a son over his own house; whose house are we, if we hold fast the confidence and the rejoicing of the hope firm unto the end.

Wherefore (as the Holy Ghost saith, To day if ye will hear his voice,

Harden not your hearts, as in the provocation, in the day of temptation in the wilderness:

When your fathers tempted me, proved me, and saw my works forty years.

Wherefore I was grieved with that generation, and said, They do alway err in their heart; and they have not known my ways.

So I sware in my wrath, They shall not enter into my rest.)

Take heed, brethren, lest there be in any of you an evil heart of unbelief, in departing from the living God.

But exhort one another daily, while it is called To day; lest any of you be hardened through the deceitfulness of sin.

For we are made partakers of Christ, if we hold the beginning of our confidence stedfast unto the end.

—*Hebrews 3:6–14*

Be sober, be vigilant; because your adversary the devil, as a roaring lion, walketh about, seeking whom he may devour:

Whom resist stedfast in the faith, knowing that the same afflictions are accomplished in your brethren that are in the world.

—1 Peter 5:8–9

These Women Made Excellent Decisions . . .

The block of granite which was an obstacle in the pathway of the weak becomes a stepping-stone in the pathway of the strong.

—Thomas Carlyle

ᘓ Rahab

And the king of Jericho sent unto Rahab, saying, Bring forth the men that are come to thee, which are entered into thine house: for they be come to search out all the country.

And the woman took the two men, and hid them, and said thus, There came men unto me, but I wist not whence they were:

And it came to pass about the time of shutting of the gate, when it was dark, that the men went out: whither the men went I wot not: pursue after them quickly; for ye shall overtake them.

But she had brought them up to the roof of the house, and hid them with the stalks of flax, which she had laid in order upon the roof.

And the men pursued after them the way to Jordan unto the fords: and as soon as they which pursued after them were gone out, they shut the gate.

And before they were laid down, she came up unto them upon the roof;

And she said unto the men, I know that the LORD hath given you the land, and that your terror is fallen upon us, and that all the inhabitants of the land faint because of you.

For we have heard how the LORD dried up the water of the Red sea for you, when ye came out of Egypt; and what ye did unto the two kings of the Amorites, that were on the other side Jordan, Sihon and Og, whom ye utterly destroyed.

And as soon as we had heard these things, our hearts did melt, neither did there remain any more courage in any man, because of you: for the LORD your God, he is God in heaven above, and in earth beneath.

Now therefore, I pray you, swear unto me by the LORD, since I have shewed you kindness, that ye will also shew kindness unto my father's house, and give me a true token:

And that ye will save alive my father, and my mother, and my brethren, and my sisters, and all that they have, and deliver our lives from death.

And the men answered her, Our life for your's, if ye utter not this our business. And it shall be, when the LORD hath given us the land, that we will deal kindly and truly with thee.

Then she let them down by a cord through the window: for her house was upon the town wall, and she dwelt upon the wall.

—Joshua 2:3–15

But Joshua had said unto the two men that had spied out the country, Go into the harlot's house, and bring out thence the woman, and all that she hath, as ye sware unto her.

And the young men that were spies went in, and brought out Rahab, and her father, and her mother, and her brethren, and all that she had; and they brought out all her kindred, and left them without the camp of Israel.

And they burnt the city with fire, and all that was therein: only the silver, and the gold, and the vessels of brass and of iron, they put into the treasury of the house of the LORD.

And Joshua saved Rahab the harlot alive, and her father's household, and all that she had; and she dwelleth in Israel even unto this day; because she hid the messengers, which Joshua sent to spy out Jericho.

—Joshua 6:22–25

By faith the harlot Rahab perished not with them that believed not, when she had received the spies with peace.

—Hebrews 11:31

ℭ Abigail

But one of the young men told Abigail, Nabal's wife, saying, Behold, David sent messengers out of the wilderness to salute our master; and he railed on them.

But the men were very good unto us, and we were not hurt, neither missed we any thing, as long as we were conversant with them, when we were in the fields:

They were a wall unto us both by night and day, all the while we were with them keeping the sheep.

Now therefore know and consider what thou wilt do; for evil is determined against our master, and against all his household: for he is such a son of Belial, that a man cannot speak to him.

Then Abigail made haste, and took two hundred loaves, and two bottles of wine, and five sheep ready dressed, and five measures of parched corn, and an hundred clusters of raisins, and two hundred cakes of figs, and laid them on asses.

And she said unto her servants, Go on before me; behold, I come after you. But she told not her husband Nabal.

And it was so, as she rode on the ass, that she came down by the covert of the hill, and, behold, David and his men came down against her; and she met them.

Now David had said, Surely in vain have I kept all that this fellow hath in the wilderness, so that nothing was missed of all that pertained unto him: and he hath requited me evil for good.

So and more also do God unto the enemies of David, if I leave of all that pertain to him by the morning light any that pisseth against the wall.

And when Abigail saw David, she hasted, and lighted off the ass, and fell before David on her face, and bowed herself to the ground,

And fell at his feet, and said, Upon me, my lord, upon me let this iniquity be: and let thine handmaid, I pray thee, speak in thine audience, and hear the words of thine handmaid.

Let not my lord, I pray thee, regard this man of Belial, even Nabal: for as his name is, so is he; Nabal is his name, and folly is with him: but I thine handmaid saw not the young men of my lord, whom thou didst send.

Now therefore, my lord, as the LORD liveth, and as thy soul liveth, seeing the LORD hath withholden thee from coming to shed blood, and from avenging thyself with thine own hand, now let thine enemies, and they that seek evil to my lord, be as Nabal.

And now this blessing which thine handmaid hath brought unto my lord, let it even be given unto the young men that follow my lord.

I pray thee, forgive the trespass of thine handmaid: for the LORD will certainly make my lord a sure house; because my lord fighteth the battles of the LORD, and evil hath not been found in thee all thy days.

Yet a man is risen to pursue thee, and to seek thy soul: but the soul of my lord shall be bound in the bundle of life with the LORD thy God; and the souls of thine enemies, them shall he sling out, as out of the middle of a sling.

And it shall come to pass, when the LORD shall have done to my lord according to all the good that he hath spoken concerning thee, and shall have appointed thee ruler over Israel;

That this shall be no grief unto thee, nor offence of heart unto my lord, either that thou hast shed blood causeless, or that my lord hath avenged himself: but when the LORD shall have dealt well with my lord, then remember thine handmaid.

And David said to Abigail, Blessed be the LORD God of Israel, which sent thee this day to meet me.

—*1 Samuel 25:14–32*

But These Women Made Bad Choices . . .

In literature, as in love, we are astonished at the choice made by other people.

—*André Maurois*

✺ *Jezebel*

And I will make the house of Ahab like the house of Jeroboam the son of Nebat, and like the house of Baasha the son of Ahijah:

And the dogs shall eat Jezebel in the portion of Jezreel, and there shall be none to bury her. And he opened the door, and fled. . . .

[Then] Joram king of Israel and Ahaziah king of Judah went out, each in his chariot, and they went out against Jehu, and met him in the portion of Naboth the Jezreelite.

And it came to pass, when Joram saw Jehu, that he said, Is it peace, Jehu? And he answered, What peace, so long as the whoredoms of thy mother Jezebel and her witchcrafts are so many?

And Joram turned his hands, and fled, and said to Ahaziah, There is treachery, O Ahaziah. . . .

And in the eleventh year of Joram the son of Ahab began Ahaziah to reign over Judah.

And when Jehu was come to Jezreel, Jezebel heard of it; and she painted her face, and tired her head, and looked out at a window.

And as Jehu entered in at the gate, she said, Had Zimri peace, who slew his master?

And he lifted up his face to the window, and said, Who is on my side? who? And there looked out to him two or three eunuchs.

And he said, Throw her down. So they threw her down: and some of her blood was sprinkled on the wall, and on the horses: and he trode her under foot.

And when he was come in, he did eat and drink, and said, Go, see now this cursed woman, and bury her: for she is a king's daughter.

And they went to bury her: but they found no more of her than the skull, and the feet, and the palms of her hands.

Wherefore they came again, and told him. And he said, This is the word of the LORD, which he spake by his servant Elijah the Tishbite, saying, In the portion of Jezreel shall dogs eat the flesh of Jezebel:

And the carcase of Jezebel shall be as dung upon the face of the field in the portion of Jezreel; so that they shall not say, This is Jezebel.

—2 Kings 9:9–10, 21–23, 29–37

❦ Sapphira

But a certain man named Ananias, with Sapphira his wife, sold a possession,

And kept back part of the price, his wife also being privy to it, and brought a certain part, and laid it at the apostles' feet.

But Peter said, Ananias, why hath Satan filled thine heart to lie to the Holy Ghost, and to keep back part of the price of the land?

Whiles it remained, was it not thine own? and after it was sold, was it not in thine own power? why hast thou conceived this thing in thine heart? thou hast not lied unto men, but unto God.

And Ananias hearing these words fell down, and gave up the ghost: and great fear came on all them that heard these things.

And the young men arose, wound him up, and carried him out, and buried him.

And it was about the space of three hours after, when his wife, not knowing what was done, came in.

And Peter answered unto her, Tell me whether ye sold the land for so much? And she said, Yea, for so much.

Then Peter said unto her, How is it that ye have agreed together to tempt the Spirit of the Lord? behold, the feet of them which have buried thy husband are at the door, and shall carry thee out.

Then fell she down straightway at his feet, and yielded up the ghost: and the young men came in, and found her dead, and, carrying her forth, buried her by her husband.

And great fear came upon all the church, and upon as many as heard these things.

—*Acts 5:1–11*

Remember: Your Future Is in God's Hands!

This world is not conclusion.
A sequel stands beyond—
Invisible, as music—
But positive, as sound.

—*Emily Dickinson*

As it is written, Eye hath not seen, nor ear heard, neither have entered into the heart of man, the things which God hath prepared for them that love him.

—*1 Corinthians 2:9*

Behold, I shew you a mystery; We shall not all sleep, but we shall all be changed,

In a moment, in the twinkling of an eye, at the last trump: for the trumpet shall sound, and the dead shall be raised incorruptible, and we shall be changed.

For this corruptible must put on incorruption, and this mortal must put on immortality.

So when this corruptible shall have put on incorruption, and this mortal shall have put on immortality, then shall be brought to pass the saying that is written, Death is swallowed up in victory.

O death, where is thy sting? O grave, where is thy victory?

The sting of death is sin; and the strength of sin is the law.

But thanks be to God, which giveth us the victory through our Lord Jesus Christ.

Therefore, my beloved brethren, be ye stedfast, unmoveable, always abounding in the work of the Lord, forasmuch as ye know that your labour is not in vain in the Lord.

—1 Corinthians 15:51–58

It is a faithful saying: For if we be dead with him, we shall also live with him:

If we suffer, we shall also reign with him: if we deny him, he also will deny us:

If we believe not, yet he abideth faithful: he cannot deny himself.

—2 Timothy 2:11–13

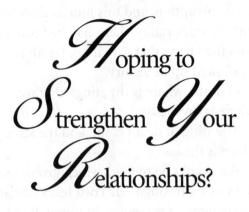

Seven

Hoping to Strengthen Your Relationships?

*W*hat does it take to keep things humming along in a relationship? Maybe you've developed some great answers and perfected a few favorite techniques. But have you checked out what the Bible has to say about it? Read on.

First, Be a Good Listener

Listening, not imitation, may be the sincerest form of flattery. . . . If you want to influence someone, listen to what he says. . . . When he finishes talking, ask him about any points that you do not understand. Then tell him what it is you want and point out the areas where you are in agreement and those where you do not agree. He will be flattered that you have listened intently, that you take him seriously, and that you truly want to understand his position.

—Dr. Joyce Brothers[1]

I pray thee, hear my speeches, and hearken to all my words.

Behold, now I have opened my mouth, my tongue hath spoken in my mouth.

My words shall be of the uprightness of my heart: and my lips shall utter knowledge clearly.

The spirit of God hath made me, and the breath of the Almighty hath given me life.

—Job 33:1–4

We were gentle among you, even as a nurse cherisheth her children.

—*1 Thessalonians 2:7*

And Samuel said unto all Israel, Behold, I have hearkened unto your voice in all that ye said unto me, and have made a king over you.

And now, behold, the king walketh before you: and I am old and grayheaded; and, behold, my sons are with you: and I have walked before you from my childhood unto this day.

Behold, here I am: witness against me before the LORD, and before his anointed: whose ox have I taken? or whose ass have I taken? or whom have I defrauded? whom have I oppressed? or of whose hand have I received any bribe to blind mine eyes therewith? and I will restore it you.

And they said, Thou hast not defrauded us, nor oppressed us, neither hast thou taken ought of any man's hand.

And he said unto them, The LORD is witness against you, and his anointed is witness this day, that ye have not found ought in my hand. And they answered, He is witness.

—*1 Samuel 12:1–5*

The heart of the prudent getteth knowledge; and the ear of the wise seeketh knowledge.

—*Proverbs 18:15*

Speak the Truth in All Conversations

> *Let not your tongue say what*
> *your head may pay for.*
>
> —*Italian proverb*

A word spoken in due season, how good is it!

—*Proverbs 15:23*

But speaking the truth in love, may grow up into him in all things, which is the head, even Christ:

From whom the whole body fitly joined together and compacted by that which every joint supplieth, according to the effectual working in the measure of every part, maketh increase of the body unto the edifying of itself in love.

—*Ephesians 4:15–16*

Speaking to yourselves in psalms and hymns and spiritual songs, singing and making melody in your heart to the Lord;

Giving thanks always for all things unto God and the Father in the name of our Lord Jesus Christ.

—*Ephesians 5:19–20*

Prove Yourself Trustworthy in Everything

Nothing is more noble, nothing more venerable than fidelity. Faithfulness and truth are the most sacred excellences and endowments of the human mind.

—*Cicero*

If a man shall steal an ox, or a sheep, and kill it, or sell it; he shall restore five oxen for an ox, and four sheep for a sheep.

If a thief be found breaking up, and be smitten that he die, there shall no blood be shed for him.

If the sun be risen upon him, there shall be blood shed for him; for he should make full restitution: if he have nothing, then he shall be sold for his theft.

If the theft be certainly found in his hand alive, whether it be ox, or ass, or sheep; he shall restore double.

If a man shall cause a field or vineyard to be eaten, and shall put in his beast, and shall feed in another man's field; of the best of his own field, and of the best of his own vineyard, shall he make restitution.

If fire break out, and catch in thorns, so that the stacks of corn, or the standing corn, or the field, be consumed therewith; he that kindled the fire shall surely make restitution.

If a man shall deliver unto his neighbour money or stuff to keep, and it be stolen out of the man's house; if the thief be found, let him pay double.

If the thief be not found, then the master of the house shall be brought unto the judges, to see whether he have put his hand unto his neighbour's goods.

For all manner of trespass, whether it be for ox, for ass, for sheep, for raiment, or for any manner of lost thing, which another challengeth to be his, the cause of both parties shall come before the judges; and whom the judges shall condemn, he shall pay double unto his neighbour.

If a man deliver unto his neighbour an ass, or an ox, or a sheep, or any beast, to keep; and it die, or be hurt, or driven away, no man seeing it:

Then shall an oath of the LORD be between them both, that he hath not put his hand unto his neighbour's goods; and the owner of it shall accept thereof, and he shall not make it good.

And if it be stolen from him, he shall make restitution unto the owner thereof.

If it be torn in pieces, then let him bring it for witness, and he shall not make good that which was torn.

And if a man borrow ought of his neighbour, and it be hurt, or die, the owner thereof being not with it, he shall surely make it good.

But if the owner thereof be with it, he shall not make it good: if it be an hired thing, it came for his hire.

—*Exodus 22:1–15*

For the grace of God that bringeth salvation hath appeared to all men,

Teaching us that, denying ungodliness and worldly lusts, we should live soberly, righteously, and godly, in this present world.

—*Titus 2:11–12*

Be Willing to Work Together with Others

When Christians take counsel together, their purpose . . . should not be to ascertain what

is the mind of the majority, but what is the mind of the Holy Spirit—something which may be quite different.

—*Margaret Hilda Thatcher*[2]

And this I pray, that your love may abound yet more and more in knowledge and in all judgment.

—*Philippians 1:9*

Two are better than one; because they have a good reward for their labour.

For if they fall, the one will lift up his fellow: but woe to him that is alone when he falleth; for he hath not another to help him up.

Again, if two lie together, then they have heat: but how can one be warm alone?

And if one prevail against him, two shall withstand him; and a threefold cord is not quickly broken.

—*Ecclesiastes 4:9–12*

And Reuben heard it, and he delivered him out of their hands; and said, Let us not kill him.

And Reuben said unto them, Shed no blood, but cast him into this pit that is in the wilderness, and lay no hand upon him; that he might rid him out of their hands, to deliver him to his father again.

—*Genesis 37:21–22*

And when Paul's sister's son heard of their lying in wait, he went and entered into the castle, and told Paul.

Then Paul called one of the centurions unto him, and said, Bring this young man unto the chief captain: for he hath a certain thing to tell him.

So he took him, and brought him to the chief captain, and said, Paul the prisoner called me unto him, and prayed me to bring this young man unto thee, who hath something to say unto thee.

Then the chief captain took him by the hand, and went with him aside privately, and asked him, What is that thou hast to tell me?

And he said, The Jews have agreed to desire thee that thou wouldest bring down Paul to morrow into the council, as though they would enquire somewhat of him more perfectly.

But do not thou yield unto them: for there lie in wait for him of them more than forty men, which have bound themselves with an oath, that they will neither eat nor drink till they have killed him: and now are they ready, looking for a promise from thee.

So the chief captain then let the young man depart, and charged him, See thou tell no man that thou hast shewed these things to me.

—*Acts 23:16–22*

I beseech thee for my son Onesimus, whom I have begotten in my bonds:

Which in time past was to thee unprofitable, but now profitable to thee and to me.

—*Philemon 10–11*

And Keep Getting to Know Your Lord

The greatest need of the human personality is to experience God Himself. This is because of who God is and who and what man is.

—*A. W. Tozer*[3]

Be still, and know that I am God.

—*Psalm 46:10*

Whom shall he teach knowledge? and whom shall he make to understand doctrine? them that are weaned from the milk, and drawn from the breasts.

—*Isaiah 28:9*

And ye shall know the truth, and the truth shall make you free.

—*John 8:32*

What is his name? what shall I say unto them? And God said unto Moses, I AM THAT I AM.

—*Exodus 3:13–14*

☙ I AM . . . The Lord Sanctifies

Speak thou also unto the children of Israel, saying, Verily my sabbaths ye shall keep: for it is a sign between me and you throughout your generations; that ye may know that I am the LORD that doth sanctify you.

—Exodus 31:13

☙ The Lord Will Provide for You

And Abraham called the name of that place Jehovah-jireh: as it is said to this day, In the mount of the LORD it shall be seen.

—Genesis 22:14

☙ The Lord Heals You

And said, If thou wilt diligently hearken to the voice of the LORD thy God, and wilt do that which is right in his sight, and wilt give ear to his commandments, and keep all his statutes, I will put none of these diseases upon thee, which I have brought upon the Egyptians: for I am the LORD that healeth thee.

—Exodus 15:26

♘ *The Lord Is Your Banner*

And Joshua discomfited Amalek and his people with the edge of the sword.

And the LORD said unto Moses, Write this for a memorial in a book, and rehearse it in the ears of Joshua: for I will utterly put out the remembrance of Amalek from under heaven.

And Moses built an altar, and called the name of it Jehovah-nissi:

For he said, Because the LORD hath sworn that the LORD will have war with Amalek from generation to generation.

—Exodus 17:13–16

♘ *The Lord Gives You Peace*

Then Gideon built an altar there unto the LORD, and called it Jehovah-shalom: unto this day it is yet in Ophrah of the Abi-ezrites.

—*Judges 6:24*

The Lord Is Present with You

It was round about eighteen thousand measures: and the name of the city from that day shall be, The LORD is there.

—*Ezekiel 48:35*

The Almighty God Is with You

And when Abram was ninety years old and nine, the LORD appeared to Abram, and said unto him, I am the Almighty God; walk before me, and be thou perfect.

—*Genesis 17:1*

The Lord Is Your Redeemer

Thus saith the LORD, thy redeemer, and he that formed thee from the womb,

I am the LORD that maketh all things;
that stretcheth forth the heavens alone;
that spreadeth abroad the earth by
myself.

—Isaiah 44:24

ℭ The Lord Is Your Righteousness

In his days Judah shall be saved, and
Israel shall dwell safely: and this is his name
whereby he shall be called, THE LORD
OUR RIGHTEOUSNESS.

—Jeremiah 23:6

ℭ The Lord Is Infinite

And God said unto Moses, I AM THAT I
AM: and he said, Thus shalt thou say unto
the children of Israel, I AM hath sent me
unto you.

—Exodus 3:14

♋ Light of the World

Then spake Jesus again unto them, saying, I am the light of the world: he that followeth me shall not walk in darkness, but shall have the light of life.

—John 8:12

I must work the works of him that sent me, while it is day: the night cometh, when no man can work.

As long as I am in the world, I am the light of the world.

—John 9:4–5

♋ The Door for the Sheep

Then said Jesus unto them again, Verily, verily, I say unto you, I am the door of the sheep.

All that ever came before me are thieves and robbers: but the sheep did not hear them.

I am the door: by me if any man enter in, he shall be saved, and shall go in and out, and find pasture.

The thief cometh not, but for to steal, and to kill, and to destroy: I am come that they might have life, and that they might have it more abundantly.

—*John 10:7–10*

☙ *The Good Shepherd*

I am the good shepherd: the good shepherd giveth his life for the sheep.

But he that is an hireling, and not the shepherd, whose own the sheep are not, seeth the wolf coming, and leaveth the sheep, and fleeth: and the wolf catcheth them, and scattereth the sheep.

The hireling fleeth, because he is an hireling, and careth not for the sheep.

I am the good shepherd, and know my sheep, and am known of mine.

As the Father knoweth me, even so know I the Father: and I lay down my life for the sheep.

And other sheep I have, which are not of this fold: them also I must bring, and they shall hear my voice; and there shall be one fold, and one shepherd.

Therefore doth my Father love me, because I lay down my life, that I might take it again.

No man taketh it from me, but I lay it down of myself. I have power to lay it down, and I have power to take it again. This commandment have I received of my Father.

—*John 10:11–18*

♔ The Resurrection and the Life

Then said Martha unto Jesus, Lord, if thou hadst been here, my brother had not died.

But I know, that even now, whatsoever thou wilt ask of God, God will give it thee.

Jesus saith unto her, Thy brother shall rise again.

Martha saith unto him, I know that he shall rise again in the resurrection at the last day.

Jesus said unto her, I am the resurrection, and the life: he that believeth in me, though he were dead, yet shall he live:

And whosoever liveth and believeth in me shall never die. Believest thou this?

—*John 11:21–26*

ℭ *The True Vine*

I am the true vine, and my Father is the husbandman.

Every branch in me that beareth not fruit he taketh away: and every branch that beareth fruit, he purgeth it, that it may bring forth more fruit.

Now ye are clean through the word which I have spoken unto you.

Abide in me, and I in you. As the branch cannot bear fruit of itself, except it abide in the vine; no more can ye, except ye abide in me.

I am the vine, ye are the branches: He that abideth in me, and I in him, the same bringeth forth much fruit: for without me ye can do nothing.

If a man abide not in me, he is cast forth as a branch, and is withered; and men gather them, and cast them into the fire, and they are burned.

If ye abide in me, and my words abide in you, ye shall ask what ye will, and it shall be done unto you.

Herein is my Father glorified, that ye bear much fruit; so shall ye be my disciples.

As the Father hath loved me, so have I loved you: continue ye in my love.

—John 15:1–9

❧ *The Bread of Life*

And Jesus said unto them, I am the bread of life: he that cometh to me shall never hunger; and he that believeth on me shall never thirst.

But I said unto you, That ye also have seen me, and believe not.

All that the Father giveth me shall come to me; and him that cometh to me I will in no wise cast out.

For I came down from heaven, not to do mine own will, but the will of him that sent me.

And this is the Father's will which hath sent me, that of all which he hath given me

I should lose nothing, but should raise it up again at the last day.

And this is the will of him that sent me, that every one which seeth the Son, and believeth on him, may have everlasting life: and I will raise him up at the last day.

—*John 6:35–40*

Eight

How Is Your Witness?

"*I thought I had never actually led someone to the Lord,*" *said Cindy.* "*But then this young lady came up to me and said she'd been watching how I'd lived for months. She decided that Christ makes big difference in the quality of a person's life. She also asked me what part of the Bible would be good to start reading.*

"*She may not be a believer yet, but she has, in a sense, been led to Christ—by me!*"

Are You Proclaiming the Gospel by Your Words?

Christianity is not, and never has been, about finding the right combination of words! It is about encountering the living and loving God.

—*Alistair E. McGrath*[1]

That in every thing ye are enriched by him, in all utterance, and in all knowledge;

Even as the testimony of Christ was confirmed in you.

—*1 Corinthians 1:5–6*

Jesus came and spake unto them, saying, All power is given unto me in heaven and in earth.

Go ye therefore, and teach all nations, baptizing them in the name of the Father, and of the Son, and of the Holy Ghost:

Teaching them to observe all things whatsoever I have commanded you: and, lo,

I am with you alway, even unto the end of the world. Amen.

—*Matthew 28:18–20*

Preach the word; be instant in season, out of season; reprove, rebuke, exhort with all longsuffering and doctrine.

—*2 Timothy 4:2*

Whosoever shall confess me before men, him shall the Son of man also confess before the angels of God:

But he that denieth me before men shall be denied before the angels of God.

—*Luke 12:8–9*

And they were all filled with the Holy Ghost, and began to speak with other tongues, as the Spirit gave them utterance.

And there were dwelling at Jerusalem Jews, devout men, out of every nation under heaven.

Now when this was noised abroad, the multitude came together, and were confounded, because that every man heard them speak in his own language.

And they were all amazed and marvelled, saying one to another, Behold, are not all these which speak Galilaeans?

And how hear we every man in our own tongue, wherein we were born?

Parthians, and Medes, and Elamites, and the dwellers in Mesopotamia, and in Judaea, and Cappadocia, in Pontus, and Asia,

Phrygia, and Pamphylia, in Egypt, and in the parts of Libya about Cyrene, and strangers of Rome, Jews and proselytes,

Cretes and Arabians, we do hear them speak in our tongues the wonderful works of God.

—*Acts 2:4–11*

And Witnessing through Your Deeds?

Are you proving that the Christian life is a joyful, happy thing? Do you look glad that you are a Christian? Does your life radiate joy and enthusiasm? Check yourself carefully

on this before you teach it. Make the
Christian life contagious.

—*Henrietta Mears*[2]

Ye are the light of the world. A city that is set on an hill cannot be hid.

Neither do men light a candle, and put it under a bushel, but on a candlestick; and it giveth light unto all that are in the house.

Let your light so shine before men, that they may see your good works, and glorify your Father which is in heaven.

—*Matthew 5:14–16*

Blessed are the undefiled in the way, who walk in the law of the LORD.

Blessed are they that keep his testimonies, and that seek him with the whole heart.

They also do no iniquity: they walk in his ways.

Thou hast commanded us to keep thy precepts diligently.

O that my ways were directed to keep thy statutes!

—*Psalm 119:1–5*

The night is far spent, the day is at hand: let us therefore cast off the works of darkness, and let us put on the armour of light.

Let us walk honestly, as in the day; not in rioting and drunkenness, not in chambering and wantonness, not in strife and envying.

But put ye on the Lord Jesus Christ, and make not provision for the flesh, to fulfil the lusts thereof.

—Romans 13:12–14

I therefore, the prisoner of the Lord, beseech you that ye walk worthy of the vocation wherewith ye are called,

With all lowliness and meekness, with longsuffering, forbearing one another in love.

—Ephesians 4:1–2

Having your conversation honest among the Gentiles: that, whereas they speak against you as evildoers, they may by your good works, which they shall behold, glorify God in the day of visitation.

Submit yourselves to every ordinance of man for the Lord's sake: whether it be to the king, as supreme;

Or unto governors, as unto them that are sent by him for the punishment of evildoers, and for the praise of them that do well.

For so is the will of God, that with well doing ye may put to silence the ignorance of foolish men.

—*1 Peter 2:12–15*

For other foundation can no man lay than that is laid, which is Jesus Christ.

Now if any man build upon this foundation gold, silver, precious stones, wood, hay, stubble;

Every man's work shall be made manifest: for the day shall declare it, because it shall be revealed by fire; and the fire shall try every man's work of what sort it is.

If any man's work abide which he hath built thereupon, he shall receive a reward.

—*1 Corinthians 3:11–14*

❧ By Persevering in Hard Times

Laban said unto Jacob, Because thou art my brother, shouldest thou therefore serve me for nought? tell me, what shall thy wages be?

And Laban had two daughters: the name of the elder was Leah, and the name of the younger was Rachel.

Leah was tender eyed; but Rachel was beautiful and well favoured.

And Jacob loved Rachel; and said, I will serve thee seven years for Rachel thy younger daughter.

And Laban said, It is better that I give her to thee, than that I should give her to another man: abide with me.

And Jacob served seven years for Rachel; and they seemed unto him but a few days, for the love he had to her.

—*Genesis 29:15–20*

By much slothfulness the building decayeth; and through idleness of the hands the house droppeth through.

—*Ecclesiastes 10:18*

Wherefore seeing we also are compassed about with so great a cloud of witnesses, let us lay aside every weight, and the sin which doth so easily beset us, and let us run with patience the race that is set before us,

Looking unto Jesus the author and finisher of our faith; who for the joy that was set before him endured the cross, despising the shame, and is set down at the right hand of the throne of God.

For consider him that endured such contradiction of sinners against himself, lest ye be wearied and faint in your minds.

Ye have not yet resisted unto blood, striving against sin.

—*Hebrews 12:1–4*

And he said unto me, Son of man, stand upon thy feet, and I will speak unto thee.

And the spirit entered into me when he spake unto me, and set me upon my feet, that I heard him that spake unto me.

And he said unto me, Son of man, I send thee to the children of Israel, to a rebellious nation that hath rebelled against me: they and their fathers have transgressed against me, even unto this very day.

For they are impudent children and stiffhearted. I do send thee unto them; and thou shalt say unto them, Thus saith the Lord GOD.

And they, whether they will hear, or whether they will forbear, (for they are a rebellious house,) yet shall know that there hath been a prophet among them.

And thou, son of man, be not afraid of them, neither be afraid of their words, though briers and thorns be with thee, and thou dost dwell among scorpions: be not afraid of their words, nor be dismayed at their looks, though they be a rebellious house.

And thou shalt speak my words unto them, whether they will hear, or whether they will forbear: for they are most rebellious.

—*Ezekiel 2:1–7*

Although the fig tree shall not blossom, neither shall fruit be in the vines; the labour of the olive shall fail, and the fields shall yield no meat; the flock shall be cut off from the fold, and there shall be no herd in the stalls:

Yet I will rejoice in the LORD, I will joy in the God of my salvation.

The LORD God is my strength, and he will make my feet like hinds' feet, and he will make me to walk upon mine high places. To the chief singer on my stringed instruments.

—*Habakkuk 3:17–19*

Not as though I had already attained, either were already perfect: but I follow after, if that I may apprehend that for which also I am apprehended of Christ Jesus.

Brethren, I count not myself to have apprehended: but this one thing I do, forgetting those things which are behind, and reaching forth unto those things which are before,

I press toward the mark for the prize of the high calling of God in Christ Jesus.

—*Philippians 3:12–14*

☙ *By Being Responsible*

Yet they tempted and provoked the most high God, and kept not his testimonies:

But turned back, and dealt unfaithfully like their fathers: they were turned aside like a deceitful bow.

For they provoked him to anger with their high places, and moved him to jealousy with their graven images.

When God heard this, he was wroth, and greatly abhorred Israel:

So that he forsook the tabernacle of Shiloh, the tent which he placed among men;

And delivered his strength into captivity, and his glory into the enemy's hand.

He gave his people over also unto the sword; and was wroth with his inheritance.

The fire consumed their young men; and their maidens were not given to marriage.

Their priests fell by the sword; and their widows made no lamentation.

—*Psalm 78:56–64*

A talebearer revealeth secrets: but he that
is of a faithful spirit concealeth the matter.

—Proverbs 11:13

Therefore, brethren, we are debtors, not
to the flesh, to live after the flesh.

For if ye live after the flesh, ye shall die:
but if ye through the Spirit do mortify the
deeds of the body, ye shall live.

—Romans 8:12–13

And they that are Christ's have crucified
the flesh with the affections and lusts.

—Galatians 5:24

For the grace of God that bringeth
salvation hath appeared to all men,

Teaching us that, denying ungodliness
and worldly lusts, we should live soberly,
righteously, and godly, in this present world.

—Titus 2:11–12

🕮 *By Standing for the Right*

On the seventh day, when the heart of the
king was merry with wine, he commanded

Mehuman, Biztha, Harbona, Bigtha, and Abagtha, Zethar, and Carcas, the seven chamberlains that served in the presence of Ahasuerus the king,

To bring Vashti the queen before the king with the crown royal, to shew the people and the princes her beauty: for she was fair to look on.

But the queen Vashti refused to come at the king's commandment by his chamberlains: therefore was the king very wroth, and his anger burned in him.

Then the king said to the wise men, which knew the times, (for so was the king's manner toward all that knew law and judgment:

And the next unto him was Carshena, Shethar, Admatha, Tarshish, Meres, Marsena, and Memucan, the seven princes of Persia and Media, which saw the king's face, and which sat the first in the kingdom;)

What shall we do unto the queen Vashti according to law, because she hath not performed the commandment of the king Ahasuerus by the chamberlains?

And Memucan answered before the king and the princes, Vashti the queen hath not done wrong to the king only, but also to all the princes, and to all the people that are in all the provinces of the king Ahasuerus.

For this deed of the queen shall come abroad unto all women, so that they shall despise their husbands in their eyes, when it shall be reported, The king Ahasuerus commanded Vashti the queen to be brought in before him, but she came not.

Likewise shall the ladies of Persia and Media say this day unto all the king's princes, which have heard of the deed of the queen. Thus shall there arise too much contempt and wrath.

—*Esther 1:10–18*

✿ By Extending Compassion

I will sow her unto me in the earth; and I will have mercy upon her that had not obtained mercy; and I will say to them which were not my people, Thou art my people; and they shall say, Thou art my God.

—*Hosea 2:23*

And, behold, a certain lawyer stood up, and tempted him, saying, Master, what shall I do to inherit eternal life?

He said unto him, What is written in the law? how readest thou?

And he answering said, Thou shalt love the Lord thy God with all thy heart, and with all thy soul, and with all thy strength, and with all thy mind; and thy neighbour as thyself.

And he said unto him, Thou hast answered right: this do, and thou shalt live.

But he, willing to justify himself, said unto Jesus, And who is my neighbour?

And Jesus answering said, A certain man went down from Jerusalem to Jericho, and fell among thieves, which stripped him of his raiment, and wounded him, and departed, leaving him half dead.

And by chance there came down a certain priest that way: and when he saw him, he passed by on the other side.

And likewise a Levite, when he was at the place, came and looked on him, and passed by on the other side.

But a certain Samaritan, as he journeyed, came where he was: and when he saw him, he had compassion on him,

And went to him, and bound up his wounds, pouring in oil and wine, and set him on his own beast, and brought him to an inn, and took care of him.

And on the morrow when he departed, he took out two pence, and gave them to the host, and said unto him, Take care of him; and whatsoever thou spendest more, when I come again, I will repay thee.

Which now of these three, thinkest thou, was neighbour unto him that fell among the thieves?

And he said, He that shewed mercy on him. Then said Jesus unto him, Go, and do thou likewise.

—*Luke 10:25–37*

And of some have compassion, making a difference:

And others save with fear, pulling them out of the fire; hating even the garment spotted by the flesh.

—*Jude 1:22–23*

❧ By Displaying a Strong Faith in God

Now faith is the substance of things hoped for, the evidence of things not seen.

—Hebrews 11:1

For whatsoever is born of God overcometh the world: and this is the victory that overcometh the world, even our faith.

Who is he that overcometh the world, but he that believeth that Jesus is the Son of God?

This is he that came by water and blood, even Jesus Christ; not by water only, but by water and blood. And it is the Spirit that beareth witness, because the Spirit is truth.

For there are three that bear record in heaven, the Father, the Word, and the Holy Ghost: and these three are one.

And there are three that bear witness in earth, the Spirit, and the water, and the blood: and these three agree in one.

If we receive the witness of men, the witness of God is greater: for this is the witness of God which he hath testified of his Son.

He that believeth on the Son of God hath the witness in himself: he that believeth not God hath made him a liar; because he believeth not the record that God gave of his Son.

And this is the record, that God hath given to us eternal life, and this life is in his Son.

He that hath the Son hath life; and he that hath not the Son of God hath not life.

These things have I written unto you that believe on the name of the Son of God; that ye may know that ye have eternal life, and that ye may believe on the name of the Son of God.

And this is the confidence that we have in him, that, if we ask any thing according to his will, he heareth us:

—*1 John 5:4–15*

Verily I say unto you, If ye have faith as a grain of mustard seed, ye shall say unto this mountain, Remove hence to yonder place; and it shall remove; and nothing shall be impossible unto you.

—Matthew 17:20

By Committing to God's Will

Let the words of my mouth, and the meditation of my heart, be acceptable in thy sight, O LORD, my strength, and my redeemer.

—Psalm 19:14

Blessed are the undefiled in the way, who walk in the law of the LORD.

Blessed are they that keep his testimonies, and that seek him with the whole heart.

They also do no iniquity: they walk in his ways.

Thou hast commanded us to keep thy precepts diligently.

O that my ways were directed to keep thy statutes!

—Psalm 119:1–5

No man can serve two masters: for either he will hate the one, and love the other; or else he will hold to the one, and despise the other. Ye cannot serve God and mammon.

—Matthew 6:24

And they called them, and commanded them not to speak at all nor teach in the name of Jesus.

But Peter and John answered and said unto them, Whether it be right in the sight of God to hearken unto you more than unto God, judge ye.

For we cannot but speak the things which we have seen and heard.

—Acts 4:18–20

❧ *By Showing Hospitality toward Others*

He that receiveth a prophet in the name of a prophet shall receive a prophet's reward; and he that receiveth a righteous man in the name of a righteous man shall receive a righteous man's reward.

And whosoever shall give to drink unto one of these little ones a cup of cold water

only in the name of a disciple, verily I say
unto you, he shall in no wise lose his reward.

—*Matthew 10:41–42*

Then said he also to him that bade him,
When thou makest a dinner or a supper, call
not thy friends, nor thy brethren, neither
thy kinsmen, nor thy rich neighbours; lest
they also bid thee again, and a recompence
be made thee.

But when thou makest a feast, call the
poor, the maimed, the lame, the blind:

And thou shalt be blessed; for they
cannot recompence thee: for thou shalt be
recompensed at the resurrection of the just.

—*Luke 14:12–14*

Beloved, thou doest faithfully whatsoever
thou doest to the brethren, and to strangers;

Which have borne witness of thy charity
before the church: whom if thou bring
forward on their journey after a godly sort,
thou shalt do well:

Because that for his name's sake they
went forth, taking nothing of the Gentiles.

We therefore ought to receive such, that we might be fellowhelpers to the truth.

—*3 John 5–8*

❧ By Exercising Humility in All Things

God resisteth the proud, but giveth grace unto the humble.

—*James 4:6*

Humble yourselves therefore under the mighty hand of God, that he may exalt you in due time.

—*1 Peter 5:6*

And as Jesus passed forth from thence, he saw a man, named Matthew, sitting at the receipt of custom: and he saith unto him, Follow me. And he arose, and followed him.

And it came to pass, as Jesus sat at meat in the house, behold, many publicans and sinners came and sat down with him and his disciples.

And when the Pharisees saw it, they said unto his disciples, Why eateth your Master with publicans and sinners?

But when Jesus heard that, he said unto them, They that be whole need not a physician, but they that are sick.

But go ye and learn what that meaneth, I will have mercy, and not sacrifice: for I am not come to call the righteous, but sinners to repentance.

—Matthew 9:9–13

The fear of the LORD is the instruction of wisdom; and before honour is humility.

—Proverbs 15:33

Nine

Follow These Women!

Look around you for the heroes. Do you see them? You will if you look closely enough. They are the multitudes of women "doing the right thing," making truly courageous decisions, day by day. In small and large ways, they are willingly sacrificing their time and energy for others in the name of Christ. Perhaps you are one of them.

At any rate, you can certainly find them in the Bible, too—women to follow and emulate. Here are just a few.

Here's a Great Role Model

Not the cry, but the flight of the wild duck, leads the flock to fly and follow.
—*Chinese Proverb*

Who can find a virtuous woman? for her price is far above rubies.

The heart of her husband doth safely trust in her, so that he shall have no need of spoil.

She will do him good and not evil all the days of her life.

She seeketh wool, and flax, and worketh willingly with her hands.

She is like the merchants' ships; she bringeth her food from afar.

She riseth also while it is yet night, and giveth meat to her household, and a portion to her maidens.

She considereth a field, and buyeth it: with the fruit of her hands she planteth a vineyard.

She girdeth her loins with strength, and strengtheneth her arms.

She perceiveth that her merchandise is good: her candle goeth not out by night.

She layeth her hands to the spindle, and her hands hold the distaff.

She stretcheth out her hand to the poor; yea, she reacheth forth her hands to the needy.

She is not afraid of the snow for her household: for all her household are clothed with scarlet.

She maketh herself coverings of tapestry; her clothing is silk and purple.

Her husband is known in the gates, when he sitteth among the elders of the land.

She maketh fine linen, and selleth it; and delivereth girdles unto the merchant.

Strength and honour are her clothing; and she shall rejoice in time to come.

She openeth her mouth with wisdom;
and in her tongue is the law of kindness.

She looketh well to the ways of her
household, and eateth not the bread of
idleness.

Her children arise up, and call her
blessed; her husband also, and he praiseth
her.

Many daughters have done virtuously,
but thou excellest them all.

Favour is deceitful, and beauty is vain:
but a woman that feareth the LORD, she
shall be praised.

Give her of the fruit of her hands; and let
her own works praise her in the gates.

—*Proverbs 31:10–31*

Others to Emulate, Too

*Though Sarah Edwards lived in the
comparative remoteness
of Western Massachusetts
the closeness of her walk with God
was common knowledge in New England.*

—*Iain H. Murray*[1]

ꙮ Two Women Who Saved a Child

And there went a man of the house of Levi, and took to wife a daughter of Levi.

And the woman conceived, and bare a son: and when she saw him that he was a goodly child, she hid him three months.

And when she could not longer hide him, she took for him an ark of bulrushes, and daubed it with slime and with pitch, and put the child therein; and she laid it in the flags by the river's brink.

And his sister stood afar off, to wit what would be done to him.

And the daughter of Pharaoh came down to wash herself at the river; and her maidens walked along by the river's side; and when she saw the ark among the flags, she sent her maid to fetch it.

And when she had opened it, she saw the child: and, behold, the babe wept. And she had compassion on him, and said, This is one of the Hebrews' children.

Then said his sister to Pharaoh's daughter, Shall I go and call to thee a nurse of the Hebrew women, that she may nurse the child for thee?

And Pharaoh's daughter said to her, Go. And the maid went and called the child's mother.

And Pharaoh's daughter said unto her, Take this child away, and nurse it for me, and I will give thee thy wages. And the woman took the child, and nursed it.

And the child grew, and she brought him unto Pharaoh's daughter, and he became her son. And she called his name Moses: and she said, Because I drew him out of the water.

—Exodus 2:1–10

✪ *She Gave Up Her Rights*

Then king David answered and said, Call me Bath-sheba. And she came into the king's presence, and stood before the king.

And the king sware, and said, As the LORD liveth, that hath redeemed my soul out of all distress,

Even as I sware unto thee by the LORD God of Israel, saying, Assuredly Solomon thy son shall reign after me, and he shall sit upon my throne in my stead; even so will I certainly do this day.

Then Bath-sheba bowed with her face to the earth, and did reverence to the king, and said, Let my lord king David live for ever.

—*1 Kings 1:28–31*

She Was Filled with the Spirit

And after those days his wife Elisabeth conceived, and hid herself five months, saying,

Thus hath the Lord dealt with me in the days wherein he looked on me, to take away my reproach among men.

And in the sixth month the angel Gabriel was sent from God unto a city of Galilee, named Nazareth,

To a virgin espoused to a man whose name was Joseph, of the house of David; and the virgin's name was Mary. . . .

And it came to pass, that, when Elisabeth heard the salutation of Mary, the babe leaped in her womb; and Elisabeth was filled with the Holy Ghost:

And she spake out with a loud voice, and said, Blessed art thou among women, and blessed is the fruit of thy womb.

And whence is this to me, that the mother of my Lord should come to me?

For, lo, as soon as the voice of thy salutation sounded in mine ears, the babe leaped in my womb for joy.

And blessed is she that believed: for there shall be a performance of those things which were told her from the Lord. . . .

Now Elisabeth's full time came that she should be delivered; and she brought forth a son.

And her neighbours and her cousins heard how the Lord had shewed great mercy upon her; and they rejoiced with her. . . .

And thou, child, shalt be called the prophet of the Highest: for thou shalt go before the face of the Lord to prepare his ways;

To give knowledge of salvation unto his
people by the remission of their sins.

—*Luke 1:24–27, 41–45, 57–58, 76–77*

☙ They Mentored a Young Pastor

I thank God, whom I serve from my
forefathers with pure conscience, that
without ceasing I have remembrance of thee
in my prayers night and day;

Greatly desiring to see thee, being
mindful of thy tears, that I may be filled
with joy;

When I call to remembrance the
unfeigned faith that is in thee, which dwelt
first in thy grandmother Lois, and thy
mother Eunice; and I am persuaded that in
thee also.

Wherefore I put thee in remembrance
that thou stir up the gift of God, which is in
thee by the putting on of my hands.

—*2 Timothy 1:3–6*

❦ She Prayed with Power

And Hannah prayed, and said, My heart rejoiceth in the LORD, mine horn is exalted in the LORD: my mouth is enlarged over mine enemies; because I rejoice in thy salvation.

There is none holy as the LORD: for there is none beside thee: neither is there any rock like our God.

Talk no more so exceeding proudly; let not arrogancy come out of your mouth: for the LORD is a God of knowledge, and by him actions are weighed.

The bows of the mighty men are broken, and they that stumbled are girded with strength.

They that were full have hired out themselves for bread; and they that were hungry ceased: so that the barren hath born seven; and she that hath many children is waxed feeble.

The LORD killeth, and maketh alive: he bringeth down to the grave, and bringeth up.

The LORD maketh poor, and maketh rich: he bringeth low, and lifteth up.

He raiseth up the poor out of the dust, and lifteth up the beggar from the dunghill, to set them among princes, and to make them inherit the throne of glory: for the pillars of the earth are the LORD's, and he hath set the world upon them.

He will keep the feet of his saints, and the wicked shall be silent in darkness; for by strength shall no man prevail.

The adversaries of the LORD shall be broken to pieces; out of heaven shall he thunder upon them: the LORD shall judge the ends of the earth; and he shall give strength unto his king, and exalt the horn of his anointed. . . .

And the LORD visited Hannah, so that she conceived, and bare three sons and two daughters. And the child Samuel grew before the LORD.

—*1 Samuel 2:1–10, 21*

ℭ She Willingly Received Christ's Mercy

It came to pass the day after, that he went into a city called Nain; and many of his disciples went with him, and much people.

Now when he came nigh to the gate of the city, behold, there was a dead man carried out, the only son of his mother, and she was a widow: and much people of the city was with her.

And when the Lord saw her, he had compassion on her, and said unto her, Weep not.

And he came and touched the bier: and they that bare him stood still. And he said, Young man, I say unto thee, Arise.

And he that was dead sat up, and began to speak. And he delivered him to his mother.

And there came a fear on all: and they glorified God, saying, That a great prophet is risen up among us; and, That God hath visited his people.

And this rumour of him went forth throughout all Judaea, and throughout all the region round about.

And the disciples of John shewed him of all these things.

And John calling unto him two of his disciples sent them to Jesus, saying, Art thou he that should come? or look we for another?

—Luke 7:11–19

ᑐ She Fulfilled God's Promise

And God said unto Abraham, As for Sarai thy wife, thou shalt not call her name Sarai, but Sarah shall her name be.

And I will bless her, and give thee a son also of her: yea, I will bless her, and she shall be a mother of nations; kings of people shall be of her.

Then Abraham fell upon his face, and laughed, and said in his heart, Shall a child be born unto him that is an hundred years old? and shall Sarah, that is ninety years old, bear?

And Abraham said unto God, O that Ishmael might live before thee!

And God said, Sarah thy wife shall bear thee a son indeed; and thou shalt call his name Isaac: and I will establish my covenant with him for an everlasting covenant, and with his seed after him. . . .

And they said unto him, Where is Sarah thy wife? And he said, Behold, in the tent.

And he said, I will certainly return unto thee according to the time of life; and, lo, Sarah thy wife shall have a son. And Sarah heard it in the tent door, which was behind him.

Now Abraham and Sarah were old and well stricken in age; and it ceased to be with Sarah after the manner of women.

Therefore Sarah laughed within herself, saying, After I am waxed old shall I have pleasure, my lord being old also?

And the LORD said unto Abraham, Wherefore did Sarah laugh, saying, Shall I of a surety bear a child, which am old?

Is any thing too hard for the LORD? At the time appointed I will return unto thee, according to the time of life, and Sarah shall have a son. . . .

And the LORD visited Sarah as he had said, and the LORD did unto Sarah as he had spoken.

For Sarah conceived, and bare Abraham a son in his old age, at the set time of which God had spoken to him.

And Abraham called the name of his son that was born unto him, whom Sarah bare to him, Isaac.

—*Genesis 17:15–19; 18:9–14; 21:1–3*

ᘒ *She Was a Great Woman*

And it fell on a day, that Elisha passed to Shunem, where was a great woman; and she constrained him to eat bread. And so it was, that as oft as he passed by, he turned in thither to eat bread.

And she said unto her husband, Behold now, I perceive that this is an holy man of God, which passeth by us continually.

Let us make a little chamber, I pray thee, on the wall; and let us set for him there a bed, and a table, and a stool, and a candlestick: and it shall be, when he cometh to us, that he shall turn in thither.

And it fell on a day, that he came thither, and he turned into the chamber, and lay there.

And he said to Gehazi his servant, Call this Shunammite. And when he had called her, she stood before him.

And he said unto him, Say now unto her, Behold, thou hast been careful for us with all this care; what is to be done for thee? wouldest thou be spoken for to the king, or to the captain of the host? And she answered, I dwell among mine own people.

And he said, What then is to be done for her? And Gehazi answered, Verily she hath no child, and her husband is old.

And he said, Call her. And when he had called her, she stood in the door.

And he said, About this season, according to the time of life, thou shalt embrace a son. And she said, Nay, my lord, thou man of God, do not lie unto thine handmaid.

And the woman conceived, and bare a son at that season that Elisha had said unto her, according to the time of life.

And when the child was grown, it fell on a day, that he went out to his father to the reapers.

And he said unto his father, My head, my head. And he said to a lad, Carry him to his mother.

And when he had taken him, and brought him to his mother, he sat on her knees till noon, and then died.

And she went up, and laid him on the bed of the man of God, and shut the door upon him, and went out.

—*2 Kings 4:8–21*

And the mother of the child said, As the LORD liveth, and as thy soul liveth, I will not leave thee. And he arose, and followed her.

And Gehazi passed on before them, and laid the staff upon the face of the child; but there was neither voice, nor hearing. Wherefore he went again to meet him, and told him, saying, The child is not awaked.

And when Elisha was come into the house, behold, the child was dead, and laid upon his bed. . . .

And he called Gehazi, and said, Call this Shunammite. So he called her. And when she was come in unto him, he said, Take up thy son.

—*2 Kings 4:30–32, 36*

♊ She Obeyed God's Prophet

Now there cried a certain woman of the wives of the sons of the prophets unto Elisha, saying, Thy servant my husband is dead; and thou knowest that thy servant did fear the LORD: and the creditor is come to take unto him my two sons to be bondmen.

And Elisha said unto her, What shall I do for thee? tell me, what hast thou in the house? And she said, Thine handmaid hath not any thing in the house, save a pot of oil.

Then he said, Go, borrow thee vessels abroad of all thy neighbours, even empty vessels; borrow not a few.

And when thou art come in, thou shalt shut the door upon thee and upon thy sons, and shalt pour out into all those vessels, and thou shalt set aside that which is full.

So she went from him, and shut the door upon her and upon her sons, who brought the vessels to her; and she poured out.

And it came to pass, when the vessels were full, that she said unto her son, Bring me yet a vessel. And he said unto her, There is not a vessel more. And the oil stayed.

Then she came and told the man of God. And he said, Go, sell the oil, and pay thy debt, and live thou and thy children of the rest.

—*2 Kings 4:1–7*

✺ *She Answered Wisely*

And from thence he arose, and went into the borders of Tyre and Sidon, and entered into an house, and would have no man know it: but he could not be hid.

For a certain woman, whose young daughter had an unclean spirit, heard of him, and came and fell at his feet:

The woman was a Greek, a Syrophenician by nation; and she besought him that he would cast forth the devil out of her daughter.

But Jesus said unto her, Let the children first be filled: for it is not meet to take the children's bread, and to cast it unto the dogs.

And she answered and said unto him, Yes, Lord: yet the dogs under the table eat of the children's crumbs.

And he said unto her, For this saying go thy way; the devil is gone out of thy daughter.

And when she was come to her house, she found the devil gone out, and her daughter laid upon the bed.

—Mark 7:24–30

⚭ She Worked Hard and Worshiped God

And a certain woman named Lydia, a seller of purple, of the city of Thyatira, which worshipped God, heard us: whose heart the Lord opened, that she attended unto the things which were spoken of Paul.

And when she was baptized, and her household, she besought us, saying, If ye have judged me to be faithful to the Lord,

come into my house, and abide there. And
she constrained us.

—*Acts 16:14–15*

ℭ She Was Filled with Good Works

Now there was at Joppa a certain disciple
named Tabitha, which by interpretation is
called Dorcas: this woman was full of good
works and almsdeeds which she did.

And it came to pass in those days, that
she was sick, and died: whom when they
had washed, they laid her in an upper
chamber.

And forasmuch as Lydda was nigh to
Joppa, and the disciples had heard that
Peter was there, they sent unto him two
men, desiring him that he would not delay
to come to them.

Then Peter arose and went with them.
When he was come, they brought him into
the upper chamber: and all the widows
stood by him weeping, and shewing the
coats and garments which Dorcas made,
while she was with them.

But Peter put them all forth, and kneeled down, and prayed; and turning him to the body said, Tabitha, arise. And she opened her eyes: and when she saw Peter, she sat up.

And he gave her his hand, and lifted her up, and when he had called the saints and widows, presented her alive.

And it was known throughout all Joppa; and many believed in the Lord.

—Acts 9:36–42

🙢 She Led with a Spirit of Self-Sacrifice

Again Esther spake unto Hatach, and gave him commandment unto Mordecai;

All the king's servants, and the people of the king's provinces, do know, that whosoever, whether man or woman, shall come unto the king into the inner court, who is not called, there is one law of his to put him to death, except such to whom the king shall hold out the golden sceptre, that he may live: but I have not been called to come in unto the king these thirty days.

And they told to Mordecai Esther's words.

Then Mordecai commanded to answer Esther, Think not with thyself that thou shalt escape in the king's house, more than all the Jews.

For if thou altogether holdest thy peace at this time, then shall there enlargement and deliverance arise to the Jews from another place; but thou and thy father's house shall be destroyed: and who knoweth whether thou art come to the kingdom for such a time as this?

Then Esther bade them return Mordecai this answer,

Go, gather together all the Jews that are present in Shushan, and fast ye for me, and neither eat nor drink three days, night or day: I also and my maidens will fast likewise; and so will I go in unto the king, which is not according to the law: and if I perish, I perish.

So Mordecai went his way, and did according to all that Esther had commanded him.

—Esther 4:10–17

❧ She Led by Example

And Deborah, a prophetess, the wife of Lapidoth, she judged Israel at that time.

And she dwelt under the palm tree of Deborah between Ramah and Bethel in mount Ephraim: and the children of Israel came up to her for judgment.

And she sent and called Barak the son of Abinoam out of Kedesh-naphtali, and said unto him, Hath not the LORD God of Israel commanded, saying, Go and draw toward mount Tabor, and take with thee ten thousand men of the children of Naphtali and of the children of Zebulun?

And I will draw unto thee to the river Kishon Sisera, the captain of Jabin's army, with his chariots and his multitude; and I will deliver him into thine hand.

And Barak said unto her, If thou wilt go with me, then I will go: but if thou wilt not go with me, then I will not go.

And she said, I will surely go with thee: notwithstanding the journey that thou takest shall not be for thine honour; for the

LORD shall sell Sisera into the hand of a woman. And Deborah arose, and went with Barak to Kedesh.

—Judges 4:4–9

Then sang Deborah and Barak the son of Abinoam on that day, saying,

Praise ye the LORD for the avenging of Israel, when the people willingly offered themselves.

Hear, O ye kings; give ear, O ye princes; I, even I, will sing unto the LORD; I will sing praise to the LORD God of Israel.

LORD, when thou wentest out of Seir, when thou marchedst out of the field of Edom, the earth trembled, and the heavens dropped, the clouds also dropped water.

The mountains melted from before the LORD, even that Sinai from before the LORD God of Israel.

In the days of Shamgar the son of Anath, in the days of Jael, the highways were unoccupied, and the travellers walked through byways.

The inhabitants of the villages ceased, they ceased in Israel, until that I Deborah arose, that I arose a mother in Israel.

They chose new gods; then was war in the gates: was there a shield or spear seen among forty thousand in Israel?

My heart is toward the governors of Israel, that offered themselves willingly among the people. Bless ye the LORD.

Speak, ye that ride on white asses, ye that sit in judgment, and walk by the way.

They that are delivered from the noise of archers in the places of drawing water, there shall they rehearse the righteous acts of the LORD, even the righteous acts toward the inhabitants of his villages in Israel: then shall the people of the LORD go down to the gates.

Awake, awake, Deborah: awake, awake, utter a song: arise, Barak, and lead thy captivity captive, thou son of Abinoam.

—*Judges 5:1–12*

❧ She Rejoiced in God's Goodness

And in the sixth month the angel Gabriel was sent from God unto a city of Galilee, named Nazareth,

To a virgin espoused to a man whose name was Joseph, of the house of David; and the virgin's name was Mary.

And the angel came in unto her, and said, Hail, thou that art highly favoured, the Lord is with thee: blessed art thou among women.

And when she saw him, she was troubled at his saying, and cast in her mind what manner of salutation this should be.

And the angel said unto her, Fear not, Mary: for thou hast found favour with God.

And, behold, thou shalt conceive in thy womb, and bring forth a son, and shalt call his name JESUS. . . .

And Mary said, My soul doth magnify the Lord,

And my spirit hath rejoiced in God my Saviour.

For he hath regarded the low estate of his handmaiden: for, behold, from henceforth all generations shall call me blessed.

For he that is mighty hath done to me great things; and holy is his name.

And his mercy is on them that fear him from generation to generation.

He hath shewed strength with his arm; he hath scattered the proud in the imagination of their hearts.

He hath put down the mighty from their seats, and exalted them of low degree.

He hath filled the hungry with good things; and the rich he hath sent empty away.

—Luke 1:26–31, 46–53

This Is God's Call to All Women

Blessed is the influence of one true, loving human soul on another.

—Mary Ann Eliot

For even hereunto were ye called: because Christ also suffered for us, leaving us an example, that ye should follow his steps.

—*1 Peter 2:21*

If ye then be risen with Christ, seek those things which are above, where Christ sitteth on the right hand of God.

Set your affection on things above, not on things on the earth.

For ye are dead, and your life is hid with Christ in God.

When Christ, who is our life, shall appear, then shall ye also appear with him in glory.

Mortify therefore your members which are upon the earth; fornication, uncleanness, inordinate affection, evil concupiscence, and covetousness, which is idolatry:

For which things' sake the wrath of God cometh on the children of disobedience:

In the which ye also walked some time, when ye lived in them.

But now ye also put off all these; anger, wrath, malice, blasphemy, filthy communication out of your mouth.

Lie not one to another, seeing that ye have put off the old man with his deeds; . . .

Put on therefore, as the elect of God, holy and beloved, bowels of mercies, kindness, humbleness of mind, meekness, longsuffering;

Forbearing one another, and forgiving one another, if any man have a quarrel against any: even as Christ forgave you, so also do ye.

And above all these things put on charity, which is the bond of perfectness.

And let the peace of God rule in your hearts, to the which also ye are called in one body; and be ye thankful.

Let the word of Christ dwell in you richly in all wisdom; teaching and admonishing one another in psalms and hymns and spiritual songs, singing with grace in your hearts to the Lord.

And whatsoever ye do in word or deed, do all in the name of the Lord Jesus, giving thanks to God and the Father by him.

—Colossians 3:1–9, 12–17

Notes

Chapter One

1. Oprah Winfrey, in Rosalie Maggio, ed., *Quotations for the Soul* (Paramus: Prentice Hall, 1997).

2. Madeleine L'Engle, in *Quotations for the Soul.*

Chapter 2

1. Gary Wilde, quoted in *God's Daily Inspirations* (Lincolnwood: Publications International, Ltd., 1997).

Chapter Three

1. Annie Dillard, in "Pilgrim at Tender Creek," quoted in *Women's Wisdom through the Ages* (Wheaton: Harold Shaw Publishers, 1994).

2. Dr. Wayne W. Dyer, quoted in William Safire and Leonard Safir, eds., *Words of Wisdom* (New York: Fireside, 1989).

3. John Bradshaw, in *Healing the Shame that Binds You* (Deerfield Beach: Health Communications, Inc., 1988).

Chapter Five

1. Mary Artemisia Lathbury, in *Quotations for the Soul.*

Chapter Seven

1. Dr. Joyce Brothers, in *Words of Wisdom.*

2. Margaret Hilda Thatcher, in *Women's Wisdom through the Ages.*

3. A.W. Tozer, quoted in *The Pursuit of God: A 31-Day Experience* (Camp Hill: Christian Publications, 1995), 2.

Chapter Eight

1. Alistair E. McGrath, "Understanding Doctrine: What It Is," in *Christianity Today,* 4 March 1996.

2. Henrietta Mears, "Dream Big: The Henrietta Mears Story," in *Christianity Today,* 29 April 1996.

Chapter Nine

1. Iain H. Murray, *Jonathan Edwards: A New Biography* (Edinburgh: Banner of Truth Trust, 1987), 197.